WHITETAIL AUTUMN

WHITETAIL AUTUMN

SEASONS OF THE WHITETAIL
BOOK ONE

Text by John J. Ozoga

WILLOW CREEK PRESS
Minocqua, Wisconsin

10-22-12

PHOTOGRAPHY:

Charles J. Alsheimer, pp. 2, 8, 22, 36-38, 50, 81, 82, 83, 92, 95, 97, 102, 109, 111, 114, 116, 118, 124, 135, 136, 142.

Denver Bryan, pp. 5, 23, 33, 59, 68, 76, 90, 101, 106, 127, 160.

Jeff Richter, pp. 10, 12, 61.

Mike Biggs, pp. 11, 16, 69, 72, 77, 120.

Bill Lea, pp. 14, 18, 20-21, 26, 31, 43, 46, 53, 54, 62, 80, 85, 94, 105, 113, 117, 119, 130, 146, 147, 148, 150.

Judd Cooney, pp. 15, 30, 64.

Tim Christie, pp. 24, 44, 55, 74-75, 84, 140.

Bill Kinney, pp. 25, 29, 35, 40, 51, 57, 60, 67, 70, 139, 143, 149, 152, 156.

Henry F. Zeman, p. 28.

Jeanne Drake, pp. 34, 154.

Michael H. Francis, pp. 42, 48, 88, 155.

Greg Gersbach, p. 49.

Steve Maslowski, p. 56.

Len Rue, Jr., pp. 78, 79, 122.

Leonard Lee Rue, III, p. 87.

Mike Blair, pp. 73, 91, 128, 132.

Richard P. Smith, p. 96.

Bill Buckley/Images on the Wild Side, p. 98.

ISBN 1-57223-007-X

Published by WILLOW CREEK PRESS, an imprint of Outlook Publishing, P.O. Box 881, Minocqua, WI 54548

Designed by Patricia Bickner Linder

For information on other Willow Creek titles, write or call 1-800-850-WILD.

Printed in the U.S.A.

ACKNOWLEDGEMENTS

No book just happens, not without the involvement of a lot of people; this one is no exception. I am indebted to many, including those that contributed the excellent photographs that adorn these pages, and I apologize to many others not mentioned herein specifically by name.

Obviously, *Whitetail Autumn* is a sequel to *Whitetail Country*. In that regard, I'm grateful to Chuck and Tom Petrie for giving me the chance of a lifetime, and for their help in putting together a book that we can all be proud of.

One doesn't work for an organization for over 33 years, as I did with the Michigan Department of Natural Resources, without having had the cooperation of a lot of people. I'd especially like to thank those from the Cusino Wildlife Research Station: Craig Bienz, Rodney Clute, Pete Davis, Dan DeLisle, Dick Dover, Jeff Lukowski, Leo Perry, Bruce Veneberg, and Louis Verme, for assistance in more ways then I could ever hope to enumerate. To Robert Doepker, Harry Hill, and Ed Langenau, three of Michigan's most knowledgeable deer people, thanks for sharing ideas. And to Carl Bennett, Wildlife Research Supervisor for the Michigan DNR, thanks for tolerating my idiosyncrasies and for allowing me to do my thing.

As you read through *Whitetail Autumn*, you'll note that Karl Miller, professor from the University of Georgia, wrote the foreword, and that I've relied heavily upon his vast research experience. To the uninformed, in my opinion, Karl Miller is the world's expert on white-tailed deer scent communication. Ironically, Karl and I have never met, face to face at least (which is not his fault), but we've collaborated on a number of written projects and we do communicate quite frequently; I always look forward to his stimulating conversation and reading his intriguing research reports. Whitetail enthusiasts will hear much about this young scientist in the future. Thanks Karl, for contributing to this book and for helping to advance our understanding of one rather incredible creature.

None of this would have happened, of course, if it were not for you, Jan. Without your interest, foresight, and encouragement, there would never have been a *Whitetail Country* and there most certainly wouldn't have been a *Whitetail Autumn*. Only you and I know the amount of blood, sweat, and tears that went into those many years of deer research and what it takes for me to put together a book. I'm sorry that I haven't said it more often, but thanks for getting me on the right track, for being there when I need you most, and for sharing the load.

DEDICATION

Jan, I dedicate this book to you. You've given me a
purpose in life that is without equal.

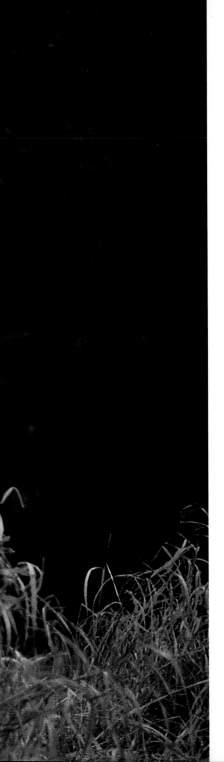

CONTENTS

FOREWORD

In North America, the lives of humans and the lives of white-tailed deer have been intertwined for thousands of years. Many aspects of Native American culture revolved around the whitetail. It supplied food, shelter, clothing and many other implements. Likewise, European immigrants to this continent made frequent use of the deer for food and trade. A rich folklore developed around the species. That folklore still persists.

During the late 1800s and early 1900s, authors such as John James Audubon, Ernest Thompson Seton, and John Dean Caton wrote of the whitetail's biology. However, it wasn't until the mid-1900s that serious scientific investigations attempted to unravel the mysteries of white-tailed deer biology. Passage of the Pittman-Robertson Act in 1937 channeled the sportsman's dollars into wildlife research and management, and the pace of these investigations increased.

In the 1960s, John Ozoga published his first scientific paper on white-tailed deer biology and management. I was still in grammar school, anxiously awaiting my first deer hunt. I mention this not to date the author of this book, but rather to attest to his long and productive career. Few individuals have contributed as much to our understanding of white-tailed deer biology as has John. Although his accomplishments represent years of hard work, for John this was clearly a labor of love.

Although John Ozoga has published numerous scientific articles, he never felt his job was complete until the information was channelled to the real deer manager—the hunting public. Thus this book about the biology of deer during Autumn.

The shortening days of autumn hold the key to a deer's survival, for if sufficient body reserves are not stored, winter's toll can be severe. The cool sharpness in the air also signals the furor of the rut which holds another key—the key to the survival of future generations of deer. AND, the flecks of orange dotting the countryside indicate that the hunting season has begun and that man has assumed a role left vacant with the loss of many natural predators. This human-predator holds yet another key that ensures that sufficient numbers of animals are removed each year to provide a healthy existence to those who remain.

This volume contains a wealth of information about the biology of white-tailed deer during the hectic days of Autumn. However, intermingled with this story is a call for the hunter and the nonhunting public to understand the sportsman's role in the proper management of the species. Hunting is (or should be) more than taking something from nature. Rather, it also gives something back—a healthful existence to the deer herd and to the whole biotic or natural community. This existence must not only be under nutritionally favorable conditions, it must be under socially favorable conditions as well. Proper management of deer means that maintaining a healthy social environment is as important as maintaining a healthy habitat.

After reading this book, I hope that hunters and nonhunters alike will better understand deer behavior and the intricacies of proper deer management. With an enjoyable text, outstanding photographs, and John's penetrating insights into white-tailed deer social life, a reader cannot help but gain a wealth of knowledge.

— *Karl V. Miller*
Research Scientist
University of Georgia
School of Forest Resources

INTRODUCTION

The white-tailed deer, *Odocoileus virginianus,* undoubtedly is one of the most adaptive big game animals in the world. Although adapted to exploit temporally favorable vegetative patches of food and cover, the whitetail thrives in a wide range of climatic and habitat conditions, withstands great adversity and quickly adapts to changes. Certainly, its large geographic distribution in the Americas, ranging from the southern fringe of Canada's arctic prairie southward into the Amazon rain forests of South America, attests to the whitetail's remarkable behavioral and genetic plasticity, and reflects its ability to cope with sharply contrasting environmental conditions.

The whitetail has not only endured modern man's intrusion into its natural environments, the species has benefited from that encroachment. Manipulation of habitats and modern land-use practices have created diversified food and cover arrangements favoring whitetails. This, in turn, compared to conditions during primeval times, has ultimately led to a sizeable increase in deer numbers and an expansion of the species' range in the Americas.

Given the whitetail's adaptiveness, it is not surprising that the species has evolved diverse physiological and behavioral strategies and therefore exhibits somewhat different lifestyles in different environments. Even the deer's anatomy differs somewhat from north to south and from east to west. Subspecies living in northern climates, for example, tend to be larger than those in the South—one of several adaptations that enhances the

whitetail's prospects for surviving the cold and deep snow associated with northern winters.

Like any other mammal's, the whitetail's behavior is the result of complex interactions between external forces and internal drives collectively referred to as "stimuli." Deer are constantly receiving and responding to stimuli from their surroundings through sound, sight, touch, and smell. Many stimuli, on the other hand, are from internal, or physiological, sources, which are generally controlled by seasonal rhythmic changes in the amount of daylight, or photoperiod.

The whitetail is constantly filtering such stimuli and responding to them while integrating into its behavioral

finding good protective cover, avoiding predators, mating, and rearing their young, even when faced with seemingly hostile circumstances.

Except near the equator, where temperatures and photoperiod remain essentially constant, seasonal changes dictate many annual events in the whitetail's life. Cycles of coat molt, antler growth, movement activity, metabolism, reproduction, and other sequences are closely regulated by photoperiod. These responses are necessary for the deer to survive drastic fluctuations in food and cover availability, and need for shelter, brought about by the changing seasons.

Whitetails are considered "short-day breeders" in that

repertoire the short-term and long-term behavioral changes necessary to survive. As do its morphological traits, then, a whitetail's behavioral adaptations eventually become genetically linked and inherited. Thus, the behavioral traits of deer in any given area can be related to certain prevailing environmental factors such as food quality and quantity, habitat characteristics, and predators.

Like other ungulates, the whitetail employs somewhat different behavioral strategies in different environments to obtain the necessities of life. Nonetheless, even when faced with seemingly hostile circumstances, whitetails are masters at obtaining adequate food and water,

a decreasing ratio of daylight to darkness in autumn causes their glands to secrete hormones that start their reproductive cycle and trigger sharp changes in their behavior. This adaptation allows them to give birth during spring when conditions are most favorable for rearing young. The selective pressures to do so, however, are strongest on northern portions of the species' range, where the whitetail's "breeding window" must be narrow and properly timed to assure that fawns are born on schedule and have time to fully develop before facing their first, and potentially last, winter.

Selective pressures regulating the time of breeding may not be so effective in milder southern environments. That is, where climatic stress is not so severe, even early- or late-born fawns may survive. In the South, even those undersized individuals that demonstrate delayed physical and sexual maturity may survive the winter season; eventually they mate and produce young, thereby sometimes helping to perpetuate a comparatively wide breeding window.

Certainly, if any one season is responsible for setting the whitetail's biological clock in the northern hemisphere, and for determining its seasonal rhythmic patterns of physiology and behavior, it is autumn. For the whitetail, autumn is a complicated and intriguing season of biological change involving complex facets of

communication and social interactions that we researchers have only recently begun to understand.

Autumn is without doubt the whitetail's most hectic season. With the shortening days of autumn, whitetails change. For one thing, they become more active during autumn—almost unbelievably so. And due to changes in hormone secretion, they begin to look different than they did during summer, and they behave differently. Whitetails even start to emit different odors during fall, odors detectable by other deer and which serve especially important communicative functions during their breeding season.

During autumn, the whitetail is in a transitional stage—the lethargic days of summer are over and the hardships associated with the winter season lie just ahead. Autumn is not only whitetails' breeding time, it is also that critical period when the deer prepare for the forthcoming, stressful winter season. And, ultimately, the social and nutritional events that take place during those few months we call autumn will determine whether individual deer, their future progeny, or even entire populations of them, live or perish.

Social Organization

The whitetail's social organization is similar in many respects to those of other ungulates found in northern temperate climates. As do mule deer, elk, caribou, and bighorn sheep, adult white-tailed deer males and females live apart much of the year. Among adult whitetails, the sexes live in separate social groups outside of the rut and seem to demonstrate somewhat different seasonal food and cover preferences. Both bucks and does show strong attachment to their established ranges, and return annually to their traditional summering grounds. In effect, they exhibit something scientists refer to as "sexual segregation," or "niche separation," of the sexes.

The basic social unit of females comprises a matriarch doe and several generations of her daughters and their male and female fawns that share an ancestral range. By

comparison, upon reaching maturity, whitetail bucks join fraternal groups comprising several compatible, but generally unrelated, bucks. In other words, as they mature, young males must leave a female societal unit and join a fraternal one.

As with any behaviorism, the whitetail's social organization originated to counter numerous environmental stresses, such as predators, diseases, adverse weather, and other factors. Therefore, the whitetail's social behavior is an adaptation—one that is critical to the species' healthful existence and ultimate survival.

The matriarchal social unit of female whitetails may consist of the matriarch, her daughters, granddaughters, great-granddaughters, and even great-great-granddaughters. Each doe in a matriarchal unit occupies an exclusive area for rearing fawns, but members of the clan share overlapping home ranges and sometimes band together as a close-knit group during other seasons.

By virtue of her seniority, ability to survive and produce daughters, the oldest doe normally assumes the leadership role and is most dominant. Other females within the group, then, generally rank according to their descending ages. This social arrangement likely evolved as a means of maximizing reproductive success and providing for an orderly expansion of a given clan's range during time of bountiful food supply.

From an evolutionary standpoint, all male deer compete to individually produce as many offspring as possible. Bucks become solitary travelers during the rut, but they socialize during other seasons. Male group size outside of the rut may be highly variable, ranging from only two bucks in very heavily hunted areas of the Midwest to as many as 17 animals in the unhunted prairie rangelands of Texas.

Among males, dominance status is determined by the individual's physical size, strength, and the experience

LEFT: *Bucks become solitary travelers during the rut, but socialize in early fall.* ABOVE: *Congenial skill-sparring precedes the often violent fights later in autumn.*

each demonstrates during bouts of sparring and fighting. Generally, prime-age animals achieve the highest dominance rank and do most of the breeding. The firm dominance hierarchy, or peck order, that develops among males within the group during the pre-rut period minimizes conflict later on and enhances social order during the breeding season.

It is important to note that competition and dominant-sub-missive relationships result in a "suppressor effect" within both female and male social units, wherein the reproductive perform-ance of subordinates is somewhat restricted. Obviously, such pressures impact the individual animal's behavior, health status, and repro-ductive abilities most seriously when deer are abundant or when food and cover resources are limited. Nonetheless, such behav-ior minimizes psychological tension and strife among individuals, encourages social order, and promotes genetic fitness within the herd.

Although scientists still debate the cause and effects of fraternal and matriarchal societal distinctions among ungulates, it is clear that male and female whitetails differ in many aspects of physi-ology, behavior, and anatomy. For example, bucks and does differ in size, shape, growth rate, metabolic rate, life span, food and cover requirements, and in many aspects of physiology and biochemistry. These factors, some researchers believe, result in behavioral traits that differ between the sexes.

Oregon State University research-ers Martin Main and Bruce Coblentz surmise that male and female whitetails select areas according to different criteria. They suggest that females select habitat that is best suited for rearing offspring. Normally, this means diversified food and cover arrangements and ample hiding cover for both mother and young as a predator defense during the critical stage of early fawn-rearing. By comparison, the researchers propose that males select

During early autumn, there seems no place for the recluse, the hermit, or the solitary whitetail. It is a time when highly evolved social rituals and behavioral mechanisms govern their fascinating actions.

Whitetails seek out and even compete for the rich and concentrated food supplies of this special season.

areas where nutrition is superb, which allows for maximal body growth necessary for the attainment of high dominance rank and improved breeding success. Among the many hypotheses put forth, Main's and Coblentz's seems to be one of the most plausible.

Clearly, because of their varying habitat requirements, bucks and does do not compete equally for the same food and cover resources on a year-round basis. This essentially means that different adaptations must have evolved in the two sexes and that environmental changes, including those involving the deer's social life, can have different effects on males and females.

The implications here are very important, particularly as they might apply to the potentially disruptive effects of modern-day deer management practices that do not carefully consider the whitetail's inherent social system.

Some scientists claim that free-choice hunting and virtual elimination of major predators, for example, have badly reduced the health status of certain whitetail populations. These scientists complain that most contemporary deer harvest systems regularly permit the cropping of too many of the prime-age, healthiest, and most productive animals (especially bucks)—mortality that contrasts sharply with the selective culling by predators of predominantly young, old, and the phys-ically unfit. Therefore, today, poor quality individuals tend to survive longer and more of them breed, thus lowering the average physical and genetic fitness of the population.

Martin Main suggests that traditional deer management practices that promote and expand female groups, especially predator control efforts and bucks-only harvesting, run counter to the population dynamics under which the whitetail's social system naturally evolved. Wherever high newborn survival and inadequate female deer harvest contributes to high female and young density, range forage depletion is likely, thereby excluding male use of such habitat. Conversely, female groups may be prevented from becoming established in areas used by males where predation or other factors reduce fawn-rearing success. In other words, Main proposes that male white-tailed deer often occupy certain habitat strictly by default—areas where no does live or where does live in very low numbers.

From a practical standpoint, however, it is important to note that seasonal segregation among the adult sexes in white-tailed deer is an intriguing and poorly understood subject, one that has only recently been carefully considered in the application of specific deer herd management strategies.

Whitetails and whitetail groups are quite active between dusk and dawn. Under cover of darkness they commingle, feed, and interact. Such activity allows herd members to communicate vital information prior to the breeding season.

For whitetails, following several months of strict sexual segregation that characterizes their summer fawn-rearing and antler-growth periods, early autumn marks the beginning of a fascinating period of social integration—a time of mixing and complex social interaction.

Early autumn is a time when the whitetail's nutritional needs change, when patterns of deer range use change, and when the whitetail's social habits and use of space change. It's that time of year when deer can be seen, often in large, mixed congregations, especially in open areas of choice forage, where they intermingle, interact, and communicate as all social beings must occasionally do.

The appearance of bucks, does, and fawns in mixed groups signals the arrival of whitetail autumn. If in doubt, the first showing of bucks carrying velvet-free, hardened antlers assures even the most casual naturalist that early autumn has arrived. The fortunate observer might even see a buck during those few hours when the bloodied strips of velvet dangle loosely about the base of its recently exposed antlers.

Throughout the species' range, the older, mature bucks are the first to rub off antler velvet, generally during the first week of September. Occasionally, however, especially on northern range, some bucks might polish their antlers during the last week of August. In southern states like Mississippi, on the other hand, bucks may not rub velvet until late September or early October.

Complete mineralization of the buck's antlers, which culminates in drying and stripping of the velvet, is cued by a decrease in photo-period, which triggers rising levels of testosterone, the hormone responsible for antler maturation. Generally, prime-aged bucks in superior health are the first to complete the velvet-removal process, whereas yearling bucks and other less-robust, older males normally follow suit within a

LEFT: The appearance of bucks, does and fawns in mixed groups signals the arrival of whitetail autumn. ABOVE: Autumn also marks the mineralization of antlers and stripping of velvet.

Antler maturation is keyed to testosterone levels which rise on cue to a decrease in the photoperiod. Generally, prime-age bucks are the first to shed their velvet. This sequence, photographed over a period of 50 minutes, illustrates the stripping routine.

Once shed, the velvet may either be eaten by the buck or left to dangle on the brush.

few weeks. The antlers of castrates, very sick bucks or antlered does may not mature; instead, they remain velvet covered because testosterone levels fail to reach thresholds necessary to induce complete mineralization.

Deer definitely compete for rich, often concentrated, food sources at this time of year. But if deer do indeed dispute area use boundaries during early autumn—the pre-rut period—such contests are very difficult to identify. During September and early October, deer of both sexes and of all ages seem drawn to, and become embroiled in, important social events that typically dominate the whitetail's life just prior to the breeding season.

During early autumn, there seems no place for the recluse, the hermit, or the solitary whitetail. All herd members must interact, to communicate their identity and express their social status, to renew old alliances and to form new ones, to compete, and to secure a position—as high as possible—within the social system. Early autumn is a time when the whitetails' highly evolved social rules and behavioral mechanisms govern their actions. And it is a time when we can see highly ritualized forms of behavior displayed by experienced individuals and when we can recognize what constitutes behavioral maturity among whitetails. It's also when young of the year, now normally about four months old, learn what a whitetail's social life is really all about.

While there tends to be a high degree of order within the whitetail's social system, it is important that the individual deer rank as high as possible in its given sex and age class. Having high rank assures access to high-quality food and cover, which is often limited, and, among males, assures the opportunity to breed.

Keep in mind, however, that such things as social rank are not static. For the individual, social status can change dramatically from one year to the next, or even from day to day, depending upon many factors that may influence the state of its health and social relationships. Even subordinate deer can secure important benefits by achieving close social bonds with more-dominant individuals.

It is now quite evident that a specific whitetail's behavior, health status, and reproductive performance will depend not only upon its sex and age, but will hinge heavily upon characteristics of other deer in the resident population. Deer density, herd sex and age composition, genetic relationships, and other factors which might determine a deer's "social environment," in addition to the ever-powerful effects of nutrition, may have profound influences upon deer behavior and herd welfare. Therefore, prevailing social factors may account for observed differences in the behavior of deer from one area to the next and over time.

Doe groups are usually comprised of relatives, daughters and sisters, to the exclusion of other whitetails.

Individual recognition is, of course, necessary to the formation and maintenance of cohesive clans, in establishing fraternal group bonds, and for the formation of strict dominance hierarchies among all deer. Although large mixed associations of deer sometimes occur chiefly in response to concentrations of nutritious forage, such gatherings during early autumn are especially timely and suspiciously social in nature. Dozens or sometimes even hundreds of deer may gather in one farm field or forest opening while an adjacent, almost identical area will harbor no deer.

Such gatherings may consist of a number of separate matriarchal, fraternal, and yearling social groups. They usually form at dusk and disperse at dawn. During the interim, under the cover of darkness, deer will feed, bed, and interact. These assemblages undoubtedly permit herd members to communicate critical information immediately prior to the breeding season.

The matriarch's first late summer adult companions are likely to be her yearling daughters (and sometimes yearling sons, for a brief period) and older daughters that failed to raise fawns. From all indications, it's the yearling daughters and non-productive two-year-old daughters, already predisposed to subordinate social roles, that seem so compelled to seek matriarchal leadership.

When adult does experience good reproductive success but doe fawns fail to breed, the classic whitetail family group will comprise a mature doe, one or two yearling daughters, and two or possibly three fawns. Because the home ranges of related does are so closely aligned, several such related social groups may periodically unite to form larger feeding assemblages, especially during early autumn.

Whitetail does generally associate with related individuals, almost to the exclusion of unrelated animals. However, when relatives are not present, adult does seem naturally driven to form compatible primary associations comprising from four to six members per group. In other words, despite differences in reproductive success or adult mortality rates, primary social group size among female whitetails may remain fairly stable. During autumn, following rare instances of complete reproductive failure the previous season, these groups may be entirely composed of adult females.

Certainly, pre-rut socialization must represent a unique experience for young fawns, most of which, until now, had never seen a large-antlered buck. The sometimes still-spotted fawns, which may only weight 40 to 50 pounds, seem especially awed by, but cautious of, the massive monarchs, which may be five to eight times larger than them. Fawns will approach grazing

bucks cautiously, almost in slinking fashion, to sniff the buck's tarsal glands or his antlers, but remain ready to scamper back to their mother's side should the buck make a sudden, unexpected movement.

Fawns lack aggressive experience but tend to learn quickly by watching their mothers. After observing its mother challenge another deer, a fawn may attempt to repeat the action by directing an initially feeble attack on another fawn. This is learning by imitation. The young loser will frequently retreat to its mother's side, seeking maternal protection, whereas the optimistic victor will more likely look for another contender.

Young whitetails living on northern range also gain

Fawns lack aggressive nature, but catch on fast. After observing its mother challenge another deer, a fawn may repeat the action by directing a feeble attack upon another fawn. These young deer seem especially awed by their first sight of massive bucks making their appearance during pre-rut socialization.

certain benefits as the result of pre-rut socialization, which may not be as important to deer living in southern environments. Deer on northern ranges sometimes migrate as much as 50 miles to reach their traditional wintering grounds. These lengthy treks are learned; they're not made instinctively. Therefore, it's essential that young migratory whitetails achieve social bonds with other deer, generally aunts or older sisters, prior to winter, in case their mothers should die before migration, leaving their young to fend for themselves.

Observations of deer gathered in open areas during early days of autumn reveals information about deer abundance, the herd's sex and age composition, and provides considerable insight into the general health status and social well-being of the local population. Although it may be difficult to visually distinguish young does from old ones at this time of year, fawns are readily identifiable by their small body size, even when they've molted into their winter coat.

During early autumn, the ratio of fawns to does will generally reflect the herd's reproductive success. A ratio of less than one fawn per adult doe, for example, will generally indicate poor herd recruitment, due to low conception rates, high newborn fawn mortality, or both. Likewise, an abundance of especially small fawns that retain their spotted coats well into autumn (naturally

Bucks within a given area are usually well-acquainted through summer social contacts. During autumn, however, as their sex hormones increase, bucks begin displaying belligerent attitudes towards one another.

prevalent in southern states where breeding activity extends into January and fawns are born as late as mid-summer) will reflect delayed breeding—symptomatic of poor nutrition; delayed sexual maturity; or the scarcity of adult bucks, which contributes to doe estrus recycling and late breeding.

Today, most early autumn congregations of whitetails contain few mature, large-antlered bucks. In most instances, if you don't see big bucks in such gatherings, it's not because the real monarchs are too shy or secretive to reveal themselves; it likely means that they just don't exist.

Members of the male society must interact and make their visual and olfactory presence known to other herd members before the rut. Even the elderly, dominant buck—sometimes inclined to be a hermit—must "show up" to partake in social festivities during the pre-rut period.

In all likelihood, the mature bucks that inhabit any given area are already reasonably well acquainted with one another through social contacts made during the summer months. During autumn, however, the buck's sex hormone secretion increases, which leads to the feisty and testy nature of all bucks at this time of year. The dominant individual must be ready to accept challenges from other psychologically charged, rapidly maturing bucks (even those still physically inept), defend his high social position, and advertise his superiority before breeding starts.

Although bucks, does, and fawns will travel the same range during the breeding season, the congregating activity demonstrated by whitetails during the pre-rut period generally ceases about the time the first does breed. Thereafter, does and fawns spend more time in the dense cover of their favored home ranges, whereas bucks become solitary travelers. And although visual signals play an important role in communication among whitetails during this pre-rut period of intense socialization, the scent-marking behavior employed by bucks, especially at antler rubs and scrapes, will serve an even more important role in deer communication during the breeding season.

NUTRITION

The whitetail is a ruminant, meaning it has a four-chambered stomach. The first chamber, also the largest, is the rumen, where food is stored before being brought back up in "cuds" to be chewed. This system provides for rather fast food gathering followed by leisurely and alert chewing while resting—another of the whitetail's many predator defense adaptations.

After being regurgitated and chewed, food goes back into the rumen and reticulum, where fermentation by micro-organisms (bacteria and protozoa) produces nutrients that can be readily absorbed and used for energy before residual materials pass into the other chambers, the omasum and abomasum. Highly digestible food may pass through the rumen in a few hours, whereas more fibrous material may remain in the rumen for days.

Like cattle, sheep and goats, whitetails can meet their energy needs directly from nutrients consumed in food along with nutrients synthesized by the rumen-reticulum micro-organisms. But the whitetail's diet, like that of domestic livestock, must contain quality proteins, carbohydrates, sugars, fats, minerals and vitamins if they are to grow properly, survive, and reproduce.

The nutritional intake of deer on a given area will depend upon the plant species eaten and the fertility of the soils on which the plants grow. The quantity and quality of food available to whitetails, however, may vary tremendously from area to area, seasonally, and even from one year to the next within the same area.

Whitetails have difficulty digesting some plants, especially those that are highly fibrous. Even so, technically speaking, whitetails seldom starve to death. They do die from malnutrition, because even when death results from lack of proper nutrition, their rumens

may not be empty. The consequences of inadequate nutrition will depend upon many variables, such as the animal's sex and age, reproductive status and general health, as well as the season and climatic factors.

Whitetails are notoriously selective feeders. They have the ability to search out and feed upon the most nutritious plants available, especially those that are rich in protein and readily digestible, switching to woody, less-nourishing species only when necessary. Therefore, in a chosen feeding area, an expanding deer herd can systematically and drastically reduce, or even eliminate, certain preferred plants. At the same time, other plants may increase either because they're less palatable, resistant to grazing, or both. Although severely overgrazed range may not exhibit the stark, overused appearance one would expect, the land's nutritional base and capacity to naturally sustain healthy deer steadily declines with continued overuse.

ABOVE: As ruminants, whitetails can gather food quickly and store it in their rumen. Later, at rest and in safety, the food is brought up in "cuds" for leisurely chewing. RIGHT: Whitetails rarely starve to death. Even in death the rumen is not empty; evidence of malnutrition.

*Whitetails are opportunistic and selective feeders, vigilantly searching
out and devouring the most nutritious foods of any given season. Here
a doe feeds on rich acorns fallen across the forest floor.*

In some areas, though, such as the flatwood habitats of northwestern Florida, deer are subjected to inherently poor nutrition even at low deer density. The poorly drained, acidic and infertile soils that characterize the area produce browse that averages less than eight percent crude protein, which is below the level required by young whitetails for proper growth.

Even good deer foods vary in their specific nutrient value. For example, some plants may be high in energy, moderate in protein, but low in calcium and phosphorus. Also, eating certain types of foods sometimes helps the digestion of other types. Therefore, because the relative importance of the various dietary constituents will vary seasonally and according to the individual animal's growth needs and reproductive status, the best deer habitat typically provides a wide variety of forage, assuring that deer can obtain a balanced diet throughout the year.

The whitetail's food habits in autumn vary according to the geographic region it inhabits, according to soil types, and to many other variables. After leaf-fall, deer turn to eating grasses, sedges, clover, and evergreen forbs such as sheep sorrel, hawkweed, and strawberry, until these foods become covered with snow. Energy-rich foods high in carbohydrates, such as acorns, beechnuts, other starchy mast crops as well as apples, cherries, grapes, and a host of wild-growing and cultivated fruits, are choice deer foods in autumn because they promote fattening. Farm crops such as corn, soybeans, sugar beets, milo, rye, alfalfa, and winter wheat, whenever available, are also preferred by deer.

Good nutrition is especially important to fawn survival. It's essential that fawns be born on schedule in spring, experience good nutrition throughout summer and autumn, and reach their full potential growth prior to winter. On northern range, fawns must also lay away large amounts of fat if they are to survive a prolonged, harsh winter.

Like livestock, the whitetail's diet must include quality proteins, carbohydrates, sugars, fats, minerals and vitamins to grow, survive, and produce. To the chagrin of some farmers, many agricultural products fit whitetail needs nicely.

Fawns are normally weaned during late summer and early autumn, when 10 to 12 weeks old; that's when their rumen, reticulum and omasum attain adult proportions. They then switch to eating whatever natural forage the local area has to offer. For them to grow properly, however, and reach their maximum skeletal size prior to winter, they require nourishing forage that has from 14 to 22 percent protein content, with males having higher requirements than females. By comparison, yearlings, which are also still growing, require 11 percent protein, whereas mature animals may only require from six to 10 percent protein in their diets for body maintenance.

Because fat reserves can be metabolized more readily than protein for energy needs when nutritious forage is scarce, storing fat in autumn is a mechanism that enhances deer survival during the bleak winter months. Like other seasonal events in the whitetail's life, the accumulation of fat is cued to photoperiod and is hormonally controlled. It is an obligatory process, meaning that all deer are inclined to become fat in autumn.

The pineal gland, tucked deep within the midportion of the deer's brain, serves as the whitetail's nerve and hormone transducer. That is, in response to changes in day-length, the tiny gland translates light signals into chemical signals that cause hormone changes responsible for setting the whitetail's seasonal rhythms.

Scientific studies have demonstrated that surgical removal of the deer's pineal gland abolishes normal rhythms of hormone secretion and thereby disrupts certain basic seasonal processes. Without their pineal gland, whitetails still express annual rhythms, but such rhythms tend to be delayed. Instead of casting their antlers in winter, for example, they shed them in spring; subsequent antlers are abnormally small and poorly formed. Likewise, pinealectomized deer commonly retain their winter coat until mid-summer, and bucks show greatly delayed onset of neck swelling, testicular growth, and aggressive behavior commonly associated with breeding.

Normally, whitetails also exhibit shifts in body metabolism in autumn, about the time the time they molt into their winter coat in preparation for the cold months, and in spring when natural forage availability increases. Again, however, deer without pineal glands lose these biological rhythms, strongly implying that photoperiod effects mediated through the pineal gland are instrumental in setting the whitetail's natural rhythms.

Adult bucks usually commence fattening earlier than other deer. They are also the first to molt into their

Normally, prime-age bucks become "hog fat" by early October. However, the stress and activity of rutting will result in a loss of 20 to 25 percent of their total body weight in only four or five weeks.

Apples, along with cherries, grapes and other wild fruits are ideal starchy mast crops that promote fattening against the inevitably lean winter.

winter coat, usually in early September, about the time they shed antler velvet. Prime-age bucks will be "hog fat" by early October, but may lose from 20 to 25 percent of their body weight during their four or five weeks of strenuous rutting activity, and enter winter relatively lean.

Even poorly nourished fawns are physiologically compelled to store fat—if necessary, at the expense of additional skeletal growth. Therefore, well-nourished fawns will be skeletally large as well as fat, whereas fawns that subsist on marginal diets may be fairly fat but usually have a noticeably smaller stature.

Because fawns must simultaneously grow and fatten, they seldom achieve their maximum size and fatness until December. Given favorable nutrition, however, they may double their body weight between weaning and the start of winter. As a result, aside from the adverse effects of deer overabundance, which contributes to forage depletion, fawns are also particularly sensitive to unfavorable weather that may bring about food shortages for them in autumn.

In southern states like Texas, severe late summer and early autumn drought frequently reduces the availability of high-quality forage. Likewise, early snow cover on northern range may produce similar consequences. Either scenario may impair the growth rate of young

Prime feeding areas are sometimes aggressively defended against intrusion despite the gregarious nature of the autumn season.

deer and sometimes contributes to their death during the winter season.

Normally, male whitetails are much larger than females of similar age. However, as the whitetail's quality of life declines, sex differences in body size diminish, because males respond more sensitively, in terms of retarded growth, to the adverse effects of poor nutrition during autumn. As a result, male fawns and female fawns may be uniformly small and exhibit nearly identical average body weights when malnourished during summer and autumn.

Before any deer can grow antlers, it must first grow pedicles, or stumps, on which the antlers form. In whitetails, these structures usually don't become pronounced "nubbins" until the fawn is about four to five months old—generally during early autumn—at which time increased output of the male hormone testosterone stimulates the laying down of additional bone at the pedicle site.

Male fawns must be properly nourished to achieve a certain threshold body weight before the testes can produce enough testosterone to initiate pedicle formation. In the absence of testosterone or in the presence of the female hormone estrogen, no pedicles will form, and antlers will fail to develop later in the male fawn's development.

Buck fawns born late in the season, those poorly nourished during summer and autumn, or those subjected to severe social stress due to "crowding" at high herd density tend to grow small pedicles (or possibly none at all), due either to insufficient testosterone production or because of a hormonal imbalance that blocks its effect. Such fawns also tend to grow abnormally small antlers when one and a half years old.

In sharp contrast, some well-nourished buck fawns mature faster than usual. Whereas most bucks carry their first antlers when one and a half years old, some large, well-developed fawns grow, polish

and eventually shed small "button" (infant) antlers less than a half inch long. Thus, they actually go through one complete antler cycle prior to nine months of age. These generally large-bodied animals also tend to grow antlers of superior size later in life.

Doe fawns usually achieve puberty and breed only under the most ideal circumstances of excellent nutrition and low herd density. For instance, more than 50 percent of the doe fawns living on the rich farmlands of southern Michigan, Wisconsin and Minnesota, as well as throughout Ohio, Illinois, Indiana and Iowa, might breed during years of favorable nutrition. By comparison, only about five percent of the doe fawns breed in the more northern, heavily forested parts of the Upper Great Lakes region, likely due to marginal nutrition and the early onset of harsh winter weather. Where they do achieve puberty under favorable conditions of nutrition and herd density, doe fawns normally breed toward the end of the rut, after most adult does are already impregnated

Nutrition also greatly affects older female whitetails. The pattern of coat molt, rate of fattening, and the conception rate among adult does may be quite variable, but will hinge heavily upon the deer's nutritional state prior to the rut. Yearling does are especially sensitive to nutritional stress because they must still put on appreciable body growth during the summer months; possibly as much as a third of the yearlings might fail to breed if subjected to nutritional shortage prior to the rut.

During autumn, the general health status of mature does is also dependent upon whether or not they have raised fawns the previous summer. Adult does that have not been burdened by nursing fawns experience less overall energy drain during summer, molt before deer that have raised fawns, and tend to be quite fat by mid-October. They might also conceive twins, even on a marginal autumn diet. By comparison, does stressed from lactating the previous summer may not attain maximum fat levels until November and may conceive single fetuses, or possibly may not even breed if their pre-rut diet is nutritionally deficient.

Clearly, the whitetail's level of nutrition will largely determine its general well-being, productivity, and likelihood of survival. Unhealthy deer more readily contract diseases and harbor lethal parasite loads, and an inadequate autumn diet will certainly set the stage for low reproductive success the next spring; low vigor resulting from poor nutrition may even contribute to abnormally high overwinter mortality, among young deer in particular.

Post-rutting bucks enter the bleak winter months relatively lean.
Nutrition and fat levels prior to this period often represent the
difference between life and death.

DISPERSAL

While young female whitetails generally establish home ranges that overlap those of their mothers, males tend to disperse from two to 20 miles away from their birth ranges. Such dispersal movement should not be confused with the sometimes even longer seasonal migrations made by northern deer to reach traditional wintering habitat.

One-year-old male and female whitetails sever ties with their mothers and other productive female relatives while new fawns are being raised during summer. Yearlings of both sexes then often band together—or link up with nonproductive older female relatives—and travel the vacant corridors that exist between the fawn-rearing areas of their female relatives. Although some yearling males may periodically take off on brief exploratory jaunts of several miles into strange habitat, most yearlings concentrate their summertime activities on familiar ancestral range.

Social bonding among does evolves over autumn into a classic family group—an assemblage that usually excludes all males. Young bucks as above are driven off.

In late summer or early autumn, the yearling does and nonproductive older does reunite with their respective mothers and their new fawns to form the classic family group. Social bonding among the females is accomplished through intense mutual grooming, especially applied about the head and neck areas. This mutual grooming is generally initiated by the eldest doe. Out of necessity, then, the younger does willingly assume subordinate social roles under the leadership of their mother.

The yearling male may trail the family group during early autumn, but he is not readily accepted into the group. As the yearling male approaches sexual maturity at 16 to 17 months of age, he is harassed, dominated, and rejected by his mother and older female relatives. Usually, adult does employ non-contact, stereotyped forms of aggression, such as the "ear-drop hard-look" in conjunction with a "head-low" or "head-high" threat, against yearling males. The doe's head-low threat signals the intent to charge and possibly strike a yearling buck with a front hoof, whereas the head-high threat normally precedes the doe's rising on her hind legs and coming down heavily on the young buck with both front feet. In some cases, several does may attack the youthful buck simultaneously, chasing him and striking at him until he is driven from the area.

The yearling buck can sometimes avoid serious

attacks from female relatives and unite with the family group, but only if he displays feminine, submissive posturing like that displayed by his sisters. In all likelihood, however, such a subdued male will be relegated a low social rank within the family group and will probably become a psychological castrate if he remains with female kin during the rut.

Due largely to intra-family strife, most (probably from 80 to 90 percent) sexually active yearling bucks elect to disperse from their ancestral range immediately before breeding starts. Those that fail to disperse as yearlings do so when they are two and a half years old.

Dispersal behavior by male whitetails probably helps to maintain an optimal balance between the amount of inbreeding and outbreeding. It tends to minimize the adverse effects of mother-son and brother-sister inbreeding, but still allows for breeding among distantly related individuals, thereby perpetuating desirable, genetically linked adaptive traits that are ecologically important.

Many other factors, including habitat conditions and competition from prime-age bucks, in addition to domination by female relatives, also probably contribute to the dispersal of sexually mature yearling bucks. However, current evidence indicates that social pressure induced by older female relatives is the primary stimulus prompting yearling bucks to leave their birth range

before breeding starts. Therefore, a high dispersal rate and long dispersal distances among yearling males can be expected as the density of female whitetails increases. The corollary, of course, is that yearling male dispersal rates and distances traveled should decrease when young males are relieved of such stress, which has been substantiated by research.

Studies conducted in Virginia by Stefan Holzenbein and R. Larry Marchinton demonstrated the importance of maternal domination in prompting dispersal among yearling whitetails. When comparing the movements of young males raised with their mothers versus those of males orphaned several months after being weaned, these investigators found that few orphaned males dispersed from their natal home ranges at yearling age, whereas most doe-raised males dispersed as expected. Also, as a group, the orphans exhibited better survival rates, which aptly demonstrates that many unforeseen risks are involved when deer move to strange areas.

Despite the findings of Holzenbein and Marchinton, however, it is not known how orphaning would influence the dispersal habits of northern whitetails that migrate long distances from their summering grounds to their wintering grounds. There have been no comparable studies conducted on northern range, where whitetails exhibit somewhat different seasonal social habits and young deer must learn lengthy migration routes from older, experienced female relatives.

Why a dispersing yearling buck eventually settles in a given area is unknown. Because he is sexually active at the time of dispersal, however, potential breeding opportunities could be an important consideration. Nonetheless, the specific factors involved in determining where and when the dispersing yearling settles likely differ from one area to another, depending primarily upon the prevailing density and sex-age composition of the local deer population.

In some deer populations where bucks are heavily exploited by hunting, the yearling buck might readily find breeding opportunities, especially if he is a large-bodied and physically strong individual. If older males are not present, the superior yearling buck might then easily dominate other smaller yearling bucks—and even unrelated adult does larger than himself—and breed successfully. Should such a young breeder survive, he would then likely settle in the general area.

In areas where the male whitetail population is more age-structured, the young male probably has little choice but to associate with other bucks. According to Dale McCullough, based upon his extensive whitetail research conducted in southern Michigan's George Reserve: "A young male can only hope to become a dominant male by engaging in hierarchial competition over a long time period. The achievement of dominant status by young males requires outliving older, stronger males and dominating males of similar age. It is not enough to maintain position; to succeed, the young male must continually strive to move up in position. This requires that he associate not only with animals of lower rank, but also with those of higher rank."

McCullough goes on to note: "Success, as in any other contest of strength, skill, and endurance, comes from long and diligent training. A young male choosing not to join all-male groups would not be able to obtain the necessary skills to compete successfully."

Therefore, the young buck must not only associate with other bucks, he must also achieve a compatible relationship with them and gain fraternal group membership before settling in a given area. Sometimes this may not be such an easy task, requiring that the young male travel far and wide, interacting with various fraternal groups.

In any event, the hyperactive and behaviorally inept dispersing yearling buck is most appropriately referred to as a "subdominant floater." Quite likely, he will interact with various fraternal and maternal social groups during the pre-rut and rut periods before eventually achieving social acceptance and finding a new home.

Dispersing young males may join a buck group as a low rung on the hierarchial ladder. If unable to achieve acceptance, they may interact with several more groups before finding a new home.

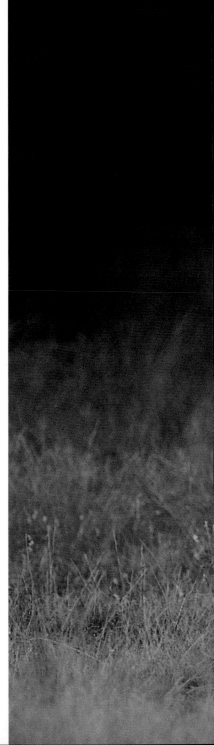

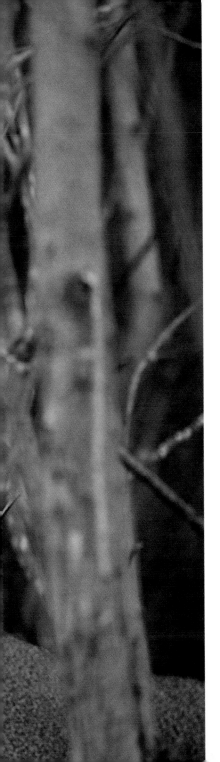

THE DOMINANCE HIERARCHY

Antagonism among white-tailed deer is common throughout the year, but the reasons for aggression, its intensity, and the specific behavioral acts involved change seasonally. Whitetails frequently clash in contests over access to limited food and minerals, preferred cover, favored bedding sites, and space for raising fawns. As with most animals, however, the amount of antagonism demonstrated by whitetails will most likely depend upon the availability of food and cover resources, which are often determined by deer density, and the animals' stage of reproduction.

Outright aggression, however, is expensive in terms of calories of energy spent and risk of injury. Although whitetails will occasionally exhibit overt aggression and engage in all-out combat, their competitive encounters are usually settled by employing highly ritualized, stereotyped threats and

dominance displays, most expertly exhibited by physically and behaviorally mature individuals.

In early autumn, a decrease in the amount of daylight triggers hormonal changes in whitetail bucks that increase their sexual drive and antagonism towards other males. Although members of established fraternal groups may associate closely while they carry velvet antlers, for example, they usually travel alone after they have shed their velvet, especially once breeding starts.

During autumn, a dominant buck, who is sometimes inclined to be a loner even during the summer months, may travel an abnormally large home range of from four

Socially bonded males may indulge in mutual grooming during the fall, but rarely after breeding commences.

to five square miles in area, likely encompassing the home ranges of several fraternal groups. The mature buck will not tolerate the close physical contact of other bucks once breeding begins, but he will interact with each of the bucks within his breeding range during the pre-rut period to reaffirm his superiority—through sparring, dominance displays, or even fighting if need be.

Initially, at least while blood levels of the male hormone testosterone are still comparatively low, bucks tend to meet in open "arenas" and antler spar in a highly ritualistic, congenial fashion. Such behavior is probably just as essential in the formation and maintenance of social bonds among males as mutual grooming is in the bonding of female whitetails. (Socially bonded males also indulge in mutual grooming, but not frequently during autumn, especially after breeding starts.) Therefore, early season bouts of sparring among bucks shouldn't be confused with the more serious, and potentially dangerous, "push fights" that may erupt later on.

All bucks, regardless of age or body size, become involved in these congenial sparring matches during early autumn. These pre-rut contests may involve bucks evenly matched or completely mismatched in age, body size or antler form. But it is the yearling buck that seems so compelled to provoke antler contact with other, often older, bucks. The middle-class bucks, generally those from two and a half to three and a half years old, seem to absorb much of this horseplay, thus somewhat buffering the alpha male, the buck with the highest dominance rank, from excessive, unnecessary energy drainage.

A sparring match often begins when one buck approaches another, lowers his head, and presents his antlers. This head-down display is almost always a prelude to sparring. At least during early autumn, soon after velvet shedding, the second buck usually accepts the invitation to spar and engages his antlers with those of the challenger.

According to Anthony Bubenik, sparring is not always a decisive contest, but it can be, and sometimes must have a loser and a winner. Bubenik, a world-renowned scientist who has done extensive research on various aspects of cervid biology, including detailed studies regarding the behavioral aspects of antler evolution and function, suggests that sparring serves two distinct purposes and can be classified either as "skill sparring" or "demonstrative sparring."

In skill sparring, a buck gains knowledge of his antlers' size and configuration relative to that of other bucks. Skill sparring is most commonly practiced shortly after velvet shedding, especially among socially bonded members of established fraternal groups or by young males of transitory age such as yearlings who are

attempting to gain fraternal group membership.

In skill sparring, bucks click their antlers together gently, with minimal pushing and shoving. Often the sounds made by clicking antlers draws the attention of other bucks, which occasionally leads to three-way sparring matches. Although these three-way encounters may be reasonably safe early in the pre-rut period, they can be exceedingly dangerous later on.

When two grossly mismatched bucks engage in skill sparring, the large-antlered buck may merely lower his head (sometimes offering only one side of his rack), stand still, and only offer resistance, tolerating the rather

FOLLOWING PAGES: The buck at left submissively "sham grazes" and tacitly yields to the dominance of buck at right whose head-down, ears-back stance displays his willingness to fight.

ABOVE: Intimidated by a menacing threat display, the buck at left breaks eye contact. Peck order determined, the two deer may then graze together peacefully.

gentle pushing of the smaller buck. These contests may end abruptly with no apparent winner or loser, and the bucks may resume grazing side-by-side. The small buck might even occasionally lick the larger buck's forehead. One sparring bout may follow another, and the interplay between two bucks might go on for an hour.

Even a friendly match of skill sparring, however, may turn into a more serious, decisive bout, referred to as demonstrative sparring, especially as the primary breeding season approaches. The purpose of these more intense sparring encounters is to assess and establish social rank. These are true tests of physical strength and skill: The contestants push and shove with all their might and indulge in skillful neck twisting, take advantage of topography by gaining the uphill side, and employ any other tricky maneuver that might cause the opponent to falter. There is always a winner and a loser, which results in the establishment of a dominant-submissive relationship.

Following one of these more-decisive contests, the loser frequently searches for another sparring partner with whom to demonstrate, in order to retain his established position on the hierarchial scale.

Within the following few weeks, bucks will repeatedly test one another. The amount of physical exertion involved in sparring tends to increase as the season progresses. This allows bucks to gradually assess one another's strength with minimal injurious battle. In the process, each buck will achieve a certain social rank and learn his position on the dominance-hierarchy scale. Yearlings also likely achieve compatible relationships with other adult bucks during these interactions, gain fraternal group membership, and thereby establish new home ranges.

Each buck then learns, by pleasant or bitter experience, which of its associates are stronger and must be avoided, and which are weaker and can be intimidated. In this way the dominance-hierarchy, or peck-order, originates, and

Initially, while testosterone levels are still relatively low, bucks meet in open arenas and spar in a highly ritualistic, congenial fashion. The serious, potentially dangerous "push fights" are yet to come.

LEFT: To observe two mature bucks, both well-versed in the art of serious combat, contest rank, is a sight to behold. ABOVE: Most bouts end without harm and without warning as one buck darts away. The victor often follows a short distance, driving the loser from the field.

While serious fighting can lead to death, injuries such as puncture wounds (above), gouged eyes, broken antler tines and torn ears are signs of serious battle.

each deer learns its place—at least for the time being—among other bucks in the fraternal group. Such social order minimizes unnecessary fighting, helps conserve energy until it is vitally needed, facilitates selective mating by physically superior sires, and assures genetic fitness within the herd.

The rank each buck earns during pre-rut sparring will, in turn, govern his behavior, determine how other deer within the local population respond to him, and determine his chances of breeding in the weeks ahead. Although only relatively few of the highest-ranked bucks within a herd usually do most of the breeding, subordinates may travel the breeding range of a dominant individual—that is, as long as the weaker bucks heed the posted warnings of the dominant buck and act accordingly, especially in his supreme presence.

Violent dominance fighting differs markedly from sparring and is relatively rare among whitetails. True "fights" usually occur only between evenly matched, mature bucks. Most fights occur about the time the first does breed, which is when blood levels of testosterone normally peak in prime-age bucks, or a short time later during the primary breeding period. On northern range, early onset of harsh winter weather may trigger deer migrations to winter cover earlier than usual, thereby drawing rutting bucks unknown to one another together, sometimes leading to vicious fighting among hormonally charged individuals that have not encountered and contested dominance during the pre-rut period.

Occasionally, two large, evenly matched, rut-experienced bucks from bordering breeding ranges will encounter, and neither animal may willingly submit to low-level, aggressive threats. But these potential combatants need not be strangers, especially when possession of an estrous doe is at stake. To observe two mature bucks, both well versed in the art of whitetail bluffing—and serious combat, when necessary—contest rank is a sight to behold.

Eye contact plays an important part in any agonistic encounter among whitetails, not only between sex-crazed bucks, but among all deer at various times of the year. Usually, deer avoid eye contact. If two prime-age bucks enter an open arena, look directly at one another from a distance and advance in each other's direction, elaborate dominance displays and possibly even violent antler fighting are certain to follow. Depending upon their age and prior combat experience, one or both bucks may exhibit exaggerated dominance displays intended to intimidate the opponent and thereby circumvent a serious, potentially injurious showdown.

Due largely to the steroid effects of elevated blood levels of testosterone, hormone-charged mature bucks

Both antlers shattered at the base from a serious fight, this buck is all but emasculated for the remainder of the season.

LEFT: Bouts can become true tests of physical skill and endurance as contestants push and shove mightily, twist their necks skillfully, and take advantage of topography to gain the slightest edge.
ABOVE: A victorious combatant, but his elevated rank in the hierarchy has come at the expense of great energy loss.

are likely to have disproportionately enlarged, muscular necks, making them look quite different than at other times of the year. This neck-swelling trait, which is generally absent among psychologically stressed young bucks, will also often enable the astute observer to readily distinguish bucks of high social rank from those that are very subordinate.

Having an enlarged neck gives the average buck a particularly massive and intimidating appearance, especially once the angry individual lays back his ears and lowers his head for a pending charge. To accentuate the threat, the aggressive buck may even erect his hair, especially along his back, making his body bulk look larger than it really is.

The two bucks, then, stride slowly, with a stiff-legged gait, toward one another. One or both may periodically lower its head and, with hair erect and ears laid back, turn its antlers slowly from side to side, as if to give the adversary a clearer view of its antlers' impres-

sive and menacing proportions. Sometimes a buck may stop and paw the ground in threatening fashion, like an irate bull, thrash brush with his antlers (an action more commonly displayed by mule deer) or emit a grunting-snort sound, signaling that he intends to hold his ground and is ready to follow up with an antler charge if necessary.

At this point, one of the bucks will usually have acknowledged defeat by stopping, breaking eye contact, and employing deceptive tactics such as gazing lazily into the distance or commencing to sham graze. Such submissive behavior commonly causes the dominant individual to relax as well, and both bucks may then graze fairly close to one another in a peaceful manner.

If both bucks insist upon maintaining their aggressive dispositions and continue to advance, though, they'll likely exhibit a "sidling" behavior. Each buck then turns his head and body about 30 degrees from the other, and they approach each other at an angle, head erect and chin tucked in. If neither

This veteran was forced into seasonal retirement after the loss of an antler and torn ear cartilage.

*A rut-swollen buck in classic threat display: ears laid back and
hair erect to accentuate his size.*

buck will back down, they then may suddenly crash their antlers together with amazing speed and force.

While fighting, bucks hold their bodies close to the ground—sometimes so close, in fact, that their briskets may actually slide along the earth as they stretch out and push. They generally keep their antlers clinched together, but periodically twist them forcefully in an apparent attempt to throw their opponent off balance. Their rapid forward thrusts and complex twisting maneuvers are surprisingly swift and seemingly vicious.

Most bouts of fighting last for only a minute or less and end without warning as one buck suddenly turns and bolts from the scene. The victor may dash after the loser for a short distance, thrusting his antlers at the retreating buck's posterior, but the winner seldom pursues the vanquished buck more than a hundred feet or so.

The frequency and intensity of serious fighting between bucks will depend upon many factors, but it tends to be quite situational in nature. Generally, more buck fights occur when deer are abundant, when the adult sex ratio is closely balanced, and when a high proportion of bucks are three and a half years of age or older (except in specially managed deer herds, such deer-population characteristics are relatively uncommon today).

Although fighting rarely leads to fatal injuries or death, broken antler tines, gouged eyes and torn ears are tell-tale signs of serious battle. But mature sex-crazed bucks are unpredictable and will occasionally fight to the death, particularly if the encounter takes place within an area one of the bucks considers to be his breeding range. Under such conditions, a battle may last for an hour or more, resulting in serious injuries or even death from exhaustion.

Should even a highly dominant buck lose such an exhausting contest, he may then be immediately attacked by any other buck in the vicinity that detects the monarch's sudden weakness and senses the opportunity to advance on the dominance-hierarchy scale. Once down and unable to rise, the vanquished buck may be literally beat to death by the simultaneous attack of several bucks. It is my view that such events lead to the final demise of very elderly bucks that are no longer physically fit and can not maintain their high dominance rank, despite their stubborn efforts.

Three-way fights can also be especially dangerous. Two bucks engaged in an antler dual have no defense from side attacks if a third highly excited buck decides to participate in the contest. Punctures in the intestines or kidney area resulting from attacks from the side can lead to prolonged suffering and eventual death of even very high-ranked bucks that are so caught off guard.

Occasionally, two—sometimes even three—large-racked combatants lock antlers during demonstration

Should a dominant buck lose an exhausting contest, he may be immediately attacked by other bucks sensing its weakness. Once down, the fallen monarch may be literally beat to death by several bucks.

sparring or push-fights. If bucks do become locked together and are unable to free themselves, they eventually die from exhaustion or from their inability to eat or drink.

Large antlers are showy structures and serve as status symbols (adornments that evolved hand in hand with the whitetail's breeding behavior) that permit bucks to display and advertise themselves and to intimidate rival males. Antlers are also ideally designed for defense while sparring or fighting, as a wide, multi-tined rack provides perfect protection for the eyes and head, and serves as a "basket" to catch and hold the antlers of a challenger. By contrast, the antlers of small yearling bucks sometimes consist only of spikes and lack such favorable traits, a definite disadvantage when a friendly sparring match unexpectedly turns into a decisive struggle.

Typically, a buck's body size, antler size, dominance rank, and his chances of breeding increase with age, and peak when he's between four and a half and eight and a half years old. Individuals of this prime age not only tend to have the largest, strongest, and most optimally designed antlers, they also possess highly polished competitive skills gained through years of experience in sparring and fighting. Probably more important, rut-experienced bucks exhibit finely tuned ritualized threat patterns and dominance displays that frequently enable

them to bluff and intimidate inexperienced younger bucks, thereby eliminating the experienced male's need to physically prove superiority or run the risk of injury.

Even physically superior yearling bucks are at a distinct disadvantage—physically, physiologically, and behaviorally—when contesting dominance with older bucks. Not only are yearlings handicapped because of their small body and antler size, they also lag behind older bucks in sex-organ development and attain lower threshold levels of testosterone when compared with older bucks. The young buck also lacks the learned aggressive skills demonstrated by rut-experienced bucks.

A buck's aggressiveness is dependent upon an elevated testosterone level. Therefore, where the buck population is more unevenly age-structured, yearlings never achieve the "psychological high" of older bucks and are more easily bluffed into submission. This suppressor effect reduces the young buck's aggressiveness and libido, thereby helping to maintain social order during the whitetail's highly competitive and potentially chaotic breeding season. The intimidated and behaviorally suppressed yearling also expends less energy, experiences less weight loss during the rut, and therefore grows to greater size at maturity before assuming a herd-sire role. This is nature's way of assuring the whitetail's genetic fitness.

Badly wounded or severely wakened bucks may succumb to normally non-threatening predators such as this emboldened coyote.

SIGNPOSTING

Whitetails are not normally as gregarious as ungulates that live in open grassland habitat, such as mule deer and elk. Instead, whitetails are considered to be more of an individualistic or solitary species, living much of their life alone or in small groups in dense vegetative cover. That doesn't necessarily mean that whitetails are anti-social. To the contrary, they are highly social creatures and have evolved the ability to recognize one another and communicate effectively.

As discussed earlier, visual signals expressed through body language play an important role in establishing social bonds and in aggressive behavior among whitetails. Even we humans can relate to, and differentiate, the intent involved in affectionate facial grooming versus that of a nasty, swift kick. And although whitetails are not overly vocal, they will sometimes emit subtle bleats, mews, grunts, snorts and wheezing sounds to accompany and enhance the effectiveness of a given bit of body sign-language.

With a forest-dwelling animal like the whitetail, however, glandular secretions and scent-marking, referred to as chemical signals, tend to play an even more important role in communication than do visual signals and vocalizations, since the latter serve only immediate, short-range purposes. Nonetheless, despite the powerful role that odors play in the lives of whitetails, even the most astute human observer will have great difficulty discerning the chemical signals deer exchange when they interact.

When compared to animals, it has been said, "…we humans have no nose." We humans can't detect odors as well as do deer, nor can we think like deer. But thanks to the extensive research conducted by Larry Marchinton, Karl Miller, and their students at the University of Georgia, we are beginning to understand more fully the mechanisms, functions, and significance

of odor communication among whitetails. Findings from the Georgia-based research and from other studies indicate that the whitetail's world literally fumes with complex odor signals that play a very special, year-round role in the animals' social lives.

As far as we know, the communicative odors produced by deer may include secretions from certain skin glands, urine, vaginal secretions and, probably, saliva. Feces also serve as a means of odor communication in some mammals, and probably do in whitetails too, but this has not been documented.

Researchers have identified seven types of skin glands in white-tailed deer that likely play some role in scent communication. These include the forehead, preorbital and nasal glands located on the head; the tarsal, metatarsal and interdigital glands on the legs, and the preputial gland on the buck's penis sheath.

To solve some of the communication problems associated with living in dense cover, white-tailed deer

The typical scrape: a buck has pawed away the surface duff to expose the soil and then urinated upon it.

have evolved an elaborate system of scent communication by establishing "signposts," which they use most effectively during the autumn period. These signposts are more popularly referred to as "buck rubs," made when bucks rub trees with their antlers, and pawed areas in the soil, referred to as "scrapes," which include urine deposits as well as scent-marking of overhead tree branches. These signs are primarily made by mature, dominant bucks throughout their range, before and during the autumn breeding period, presumably to communicate their dominance, individual identity, and other information of social importance.

Signposts are both visual and olfactory signals in that they are showy in nature and are scent marked with various secretions. In some cases, bucks might even emit auditory signals while making signposts, thereby attracting the attention of other deer. Dominant bucks also sometimes make signposts in the presence of other deer, especially right after emerging as the victor in an aggressive encounter.

Unlike other forms of communication, signposts virtually serve as an extension of the animal itself, remaining functional for extended periods of time even in the maker's absence. Thus, signposts convey long-lasting messages that likely have both physiological and psychological impact upon other (generally subordinate) deer in the area.

According to Karl Miller, "Chemical signals that relay information among animals are called pheromones. This term was originally coined to describe chemical sex attractants in insects, but has since been expanded to include any chemical produced by one individual that transfers information to another member of the same species; some researchers reserve 'pheromones' for insects and use 'chemical signals' when referring to mammals.

"Whatever the terminology," notes Miller, "these signals include releaser pheromones, which evoke an immediate behavioral response; priming pheromones, which result in a physiological response; and informer pheromones, which relay information but generally do not result in a behavioral or physiological response."

Researchers Marchinton and Miller propose that signposting by dominant bucks plays a vital role in maintaining social harmony in white-tailed deer populations. The biologists suggest that primer pheromones—those which produce a physiological response—deposited by dominant bucks at rubs and scrapes help synchronize reproductive cycles, bring adult does into estrus early, and suppress the aggressiveness and sex drives of young bucks. These are conditions which help maintain, and improve, the health and vitality of the population.

Unlike rubbing trees to remove velvet, this buck is making a "signpost" to proclaim his dominance within his territory.

A mature rutting buck, deprived of favorable tree stems, will rub
nearly any size tree available—even fence posts will do.

The hypothesis presented by Marchinton and Miller is based largely upon study results using domestic ungulates, especially sheep and goats. However, studies conducted at the Cusino Wildlife Research Station in Michigan's Upper Peninsula lend support to the idea that the presence of mature whitetail bucks has a definite effect on the reproductive physiology of does. Despite the relatively narrow breeding window that prevails at the northern Michigan latitude, confining bucks and does together during autumn resulted in advancing mean breeding dates by eight to nine days. The exact mechanisms involved here were unknown, but observations suggested that the close and unnatural confinement of bucks with does had some type of biostimulating effect and could have been due to pheromones produced by males, which induced ovulation earlier than normal.

Miller and Marchinton note that most research conducted on the effect of male stimulation on female ungulates has concentrated on highly gregarious domestic species where male-female contacts are frequent. In whitetails, however, the adult sexes live apart much of the year, meaning that they may not associate for sufficient periods to allow priming pheromones from the male to alter the physiology of the female. Therefore, Miller and Marchinton suggest: "If continued exposure to chemical signals is required for biostimulation of female whitetails, as it is for domestics, rubs and scrapes probably serve this purpose."

Currently, most deer population management strategies in this country emphasize controlling total deer numbers relative to the perceived food and cover resources available. Little management concern is expressed for maintaining populations of favorable sex and age composition—deer populations that exist in social harmony. Exceptionally heavy harvesting of antlered deer, regardless of age, is generally encouraged by today's game management policy, sometimes contributing to grossly unbalanced adult sex ratios and leaving the physiologically and behaviorally immature yearling bucks to function as herd sires at an abnormally young age.

My field research indicates that well-nourished yearling bucks can fulfill the role of herd sires, at least on northern range, by impregnating does on schedule with no decrease in the number of fetuses conceived. However, yearling bucks in my studies demonstrated a distinct lack of ritualized courtship behavior—exhibiting instead what I'd call a "seek-and-chase" courtship style—as compared with older, rut-experienced sires. Also, because yearling bucks are delayed in sexual development and do minimal signposting, they likely lack the biostimulating effects demonstrated by mature bucks and necessary to synchronize estrus among does—at least in southerly environments where photoperiod effects are not nearly so overpowering and whitetails have a long breeding season.

Most certainly, the inept courtship behavior employed by yearling bucks, and their lack of a firm dominance hierarchy in the absence of mature bucks, minimizes the chance for female mate selection. In the long run, this could reduce genetic fitness within populations wherever yearling bucks, solely, function as herd sires.

The priming pheromone hypothesis presented by Marchinton and Miller is not without supporting field data. The work conducted by David Guynn and his coworkers on the Mt. Holly Plantation in South Carolina, in particular, has demonstrated that delayed and protracted whitetail breeding seasons, characteristic of many socially out-of-balance southern deer populations, can be advanced and shortened when both nutritional and social factors are considered in herd management.

In the Mt. Holly study, the deer population was initially typical of many southern herds: The bucks had been heavily exploited, but deer density was high. There existed an unbalanced adult sex ratio heavily favoring females, and the breeding season was very late and protracted (96 days), with some fawns not being born until September.

To test their hypothesis, the researchers selectively shot deer, to better balance deer numbers with existing food and cover resources, to decrease the proportion of does, and to increase the proportion of bucks. As a result, within five years, the rut became more intense and shortened to 43 days. Breeding also occurred much earlier. Mean conception dates shifted from 11 November, in the first year of study, to 15 October during the final year.

These researchers emphasize that the resultant improvement in nutrition was one reason for the earlier and shorter breeding periods. A better balance in sex ratio also likely contributed to less estrus recycling and fewer females remaining unbred after their first or subsequent estrus cycles. However, increased biostimulation of females by mature bucks was likely also an important factor, as the availability of males to breed females could not alone account for moving the breeding season forward.

Only recently have wildlife biologists questioned how hunting-induced mortality (or lack thereof) influences deer social behavior. In turn, researchers are striving to better understand how such behaviors as signposting impact deer biology. In the process, they've learned that, while nutrition is of paramount importance in producing healthy and productive whitetails, sociobiological factors also play an intricate role. As a result, some biologists, especially those involved in promoting quality deer management, are now calling for revolutionary changes in traditional deer-management practices by placing increased emphasis on the restructuring and maintenance of deer populations that have optimal social structure, in addition to being nutritionally balanced.

BUCK RUBS

All bucks make some antler rubs on trees when removing velvet during early autumn. However, since each buck usually removes its velvet within a relatively short time, often only a few hours, most antler rubs are obviously produced for other reasons—primarily to serve as signposts for mature bucks proclaiming their dominance within a given area.

Investigations conducted by Thomas Atkeson and Larry Marchinton revealed that whitetails possess specialized forehead skin glands that become especially active during autumn. Does also have these glands, but tests indicate that mature, socially high-ranking bucks,

"Number One buck is still alive and healthy. So beware!"

compared with younger males or females, exude greater amounts of this gland's secretion. Thus, a tree debarked by a buck rubbing with his antlers is much more than a highly visible mark. Because rubbing is done primarily with the antler base and forehead itself, each rub also carries the distinctive identifying odor of the maker.

Most bouts of antler rubbing last only a few minutes. During a typical antler-rubbing episode, the buck rubs a stem with his antler base and forehead, periodically stopping to sniff, and sometimes lick, the exposed xylem, or inner wood. On stems larger than about eight inches in diameter, a large-antlered buck might only rub with his brow tines (those nearest the antler base) and forehead, thereby only producing deep scratches in the tree bark.

Close examination of a deer's antlers, especially those of a mature individual, reveals that the basal portion of the main antler beam is quite rough, whereas the upper portions of the beams and antler tines themselves are quite smooth. When this basal roughness consists of only small bumps less than a half inch long, the texture is referred to as "pearling." Larger protrubances between a half inch and one inch in length (still not long enough to be considered antler points) are called "thorns." These features not only give antlers a more massive and handsome appearance, they also give the lower portion of the antler a rasplike texture, making it a highly effective tool for debarking small trees and shrubs.

After velvet removal, the amount of rubbing an individual buck does immediately prior to and during the breeding season will depend upon his blood levels of testosterone and his dominance status. Compared with younger bucks, mature bucks, generally three and a half years of age and older, are not only the first to reach threshold levels of testosterone that induce antler maturation and velvet stripping, they also achieve higher concentrations of testosterone, which contributes to their extreme aggressiveness, attainment of higher dominance rank, and tendency to make more rubs.

The dominant buck that has maintained his superior status by intimidating rival bucks during summer will commence wandering and marking his former breeding range soon after "rubbing out," or removing his antler velvet, before contesting dominance with other bucks. It is now that he shifts his center of activity to interact with other deer over a breeding range of anywhere from one to five square miles in area.

Although whitetail bucks do not establish true breeding territories, dominant individuals do mark their breeding range with rubs that serve as signposts to advertise their presence and to announce their dominance in a given area. Bucks tend to travel a larger

A rub is more than a highly visible mark, because it is made with the antler base and forehead which leaves the distinctive odor of its maker.

autumn range when deer density is low, whereas they're more apt to cover less area when deer are plentiful. Since northern whitetail bucks are migratory, sometimes traveling long distances to reach winter range, they might also be accustomed to ranging farther and covering larger breeding ranges than do bucks in the South.

Whether older bucks are present or not, yearling bucks are more delayed, physiologically and psychologically, in entering rut condition. Even the most physically-fit yearlings are generally delayed a week or two in shedding velvet and never do achieve the sex hormone "highs" that simulate mature bucks. Since yearling bucks and even two-and-a-half-year-olds normally make very few rubs during the pre-rut period, an abundance of antler rubs during September or early October will invariably reveal the presence of a dominant buck three and a half years of age or older. And even during the primary breeding period, a yearling buck only makes about half as many rubs as a prime-age individual.

A mature, rutting buck deprived of favorable tree stems for rubbing will rub just about any type and size of tree available, or even fence posts and electric power poles if necessary. However, the scientific literature indicates that whitetail bucks prefer to make rub signposts on trees and shrubs of smaller diameter, and that the tree and shrub species they prefer for making signposts differ somewhat from one part of the country to the next.

The work conducted by Gerald Moore and Larry Marchinton in southern Georgia during the early 1970s produced some of the first solid findings relative to the communicative role that buck rubs play in whitetail social behavior during the breeding season. They found that eastern red cedar, winged sumac, sourwood, sassafras, short-leaf pine, and long-leaf pine were most often rubbed. Stems selected for rubbing ranged from a half inch to four inches in diameter, the average being about one inch in diameter.

Subsequent work by Terry Kile and Marchinton showed that bucks preferred to rub trees and shrubs with smooth bark and no lower limbs. They also found that aromatic tree species such as black cherry and sweet gum were rubbed more frequently than expected. As a result, they suggested that the aromatic qualities of the rubbed tree increase its effectiveness as a visual and olfactory signpost.

In both of the previously mentioned studies, the investigators reported a clumped distribution of rubs. That is, a newly formed rub was commonly close to one made earlier, suggesting that some locations were more

non-preferred trees like hawthorn were sometimes rubbed when adjacent to preferred species, but seldom when growing with other hawthorns in a block.

In northern Georgia, Karl Miller and his associates found that whitetail bucks rubbed 47 of 58 tree species available. Preferred tree species for rubbing included alders, cherries, Virginia pine, eastern juniper, white pine, common witchhazel, and striped maple. Other trees with low branches or warty bark were avoided. The researchers recorded buck rub densities ranging from 474 to 1,502 rubs per square mile, and found rub density closely related to the number of bucks older than two and a half years old in the population.

preferred than others for rubbing. They agreed that such rubbing functioned to mark areas and establish a buck's dominance in it in preparation for breeding.

Work conducted on a tree farm in Ohio by David Nielson and his coworkers confirmed much of the Georgia findings. The Ohio investigation revealed that the clumping nature of buck rubs may be related more to location of preferred tree species and preferred tree and shrub size classes than to other factors. Under plantation conditions, bucks commonly struck several small trees in a row or neighboring row in a single rubbing episode, which led to clumping of rubs. Also,

Certain types of rubs may serve different purposes. This short, broken shrub is dubbed a "licking stick" which may be used by several bucks.

Rub densities tend to be higher within close proximity to abundant food sources, yet rub counts do not appear to be a useful index to deer abundance.

Interestingly, in the latter study, rub density and distribution changed from year to year, depending upon the abundance of acorns, which served as an important autumn food for deer in the area of study. More rubs were recorded during years of good acorn production, when rubs were also more concentrated in oak habitat types. Therefore, because buck antler rubbing activity varied according to the ages of bucks present, as well as food abundance and distribution, these investigators concluded that counts of buck rubs would not be a useful index to buck abundance.

Aside from preferring trees with certain physical characteristics, the investigations mentioned generally found that bucks concentrated rubs at trail junctions, along old roadbeds, and in woods adjacent to open areas, especially where small, aromatic saplings were abundant. In mountainous terrain, rubs were concentrated along travel corridors such as deer trails, ridge tops, old logging roads, and stream junctions.

Somewhat different results were reported in Maine, where Merlin Benner and Terry Bowyer observed abundant deer rubs along forested edges of open fields. Twelve species of trees and shrubs were rubbed by deer; staghorn sumac, trembling aspen and willows were selected, whereas choke cherry, black cherry, paper birch and sugar maple were avoided. It's interesting to note that sumacs were rubbed often by deer in both Maine and Georgia. In contrast, Georgia deer preferred to rub cherry trees, but Maine deer avoided them.

Deer in all of these studies preferred smooth-barked trees from about one to four inches in diameter and devoid of lower branches, However, deer in Maine did not show preference for aromatic species as in the Georgia and Ohio studies. Benner and Bowyer concluded: "Some variation in selection by deer of tree species for scent marking on different areas may be explained by the relative abundance of these trees and how likely other deer are to locate scent marks on them."

In most studies, rub densities tend to be higher in habitats close to habitats with abundant food resources. This could be wooded cover near corn or alfalfa fields, oak habitat when acorns are abundant, areas adjacent to forest openings where deer find lush herbaceous growth flushed by autumn rains, locations near artificial feeders, or areas near any other type of concentrated autumn food source for deer. Such a rubbing strategy makes a great deal of sense, because other deer would also likely concentrate near such choice feeding sites, making the buck's advertising via antler rubs most effective.

My general observations in heavily forested cover of northern Michigan have been in close agreement with those from the Maine studies, namely that the most attractive buck rubs are those located along forest opening edges where deer can detect them from a fair distance. In the Upper Great Lakes region, smooth-barked trees such as trembling aspen, about two inches in diameter, with no lower limbs, seem to be highly preferred by bucks for rubs. Aspen is not only easily de-barked, the inner wood is very light colored and exhibits reasonably long-lasting brilliance once exposed by rubbing. Aspen in non-aromatic.

Given the above considerations, I theorized that bucks could be induced to rub artificially positioned stems if the stems possessed favorable traits and were located along forest openings.   I decided to test my theory in the Michigan's Cusino Wildlife Research Area, a square-mile enclosure, using trembling aspen poles. On September 24, 1993, I cut 25 aspen saplings, each about two inches in diameter, from outside the enclosure. I then cut the top off and trimmed all the branches from each, leaving poles about eight feet long. I set them in place along opening edges, using a two-foot length of two-inch diameter pipe to core a hole about 18 inches deep, then just stuck the pole in the ground and tamped the soil firmly to hold it in place.

Given what other studies had shown, and my favorable experience using fake rubs in the past, I felt confident that at least some of the poles would be rubbed. As it turned out, buck response to the poles bordered on the extraordinary.

Twelve of the 25 poles were rubbed by bucks during the first week; within two weeks, 23 of the poles had been rubbed and many had shown signs of repeat rubbing. Within four weeks, all 25 had been rubbed, and within five weeks all of the stems had been rubbed multiple times.

The high frequency of rubbing was certainly a surprise, but the repeated rubbing of the stems was even more mystifying. Generally, except in the case of "traditional rubs" (discussed later), bucks only re-rub about five to ten percent of their established rubs during the same season.

Having had 15 antlered bucks present in the enclosure, five of which were three and a half years of age or older, certainly contributed to the high incidence of rubbing. However, these bucks were also terribly deprived of choice rubbing stems. The area had no timber harvesting for over 20 years. Therefore, preferred rubbing stems in the small size classes were particularly scarce along opening edges, which likely made the artificially placed stems even more attractive.

After two weeks into the study, I set a second unrubbed pole beside each of the 23 poles that had already been rubbed. My question was: Which stem would bucks prefer to rub—one that had already been marked or a new, clean stem? Obviously, considering previous research findings, one would expect a revisiting buck to rub the unrubbed stem, thereby leading to the observed clumping of rubs. That's exactly what happened.

Given the opportunity to re-rub, or make a new rub, bucks chose to rub the new stem. However, in some cases both stems were rubbed during the same 24-hour period. Within three weeks, all of the new poles were also rubbed, and 21 of 23 showed signs of being re-rubbed. In other words, not only did all 48 aspen poles I set in place turn into buck rubs, 46 of 48 were re-rubbed one or more times.

During the coarse of these investigations I periodically positioned automatic cameras to document deer visitations to the artificially positioned poles. I was surprised to find one sequence of photos that showed three bucks, in order of increasing social rank, marking the same pole within a seven-minute period. These observations not only indicated that trembling aspen is highly preferred for rubbing, but also suggests that bucks might occasionally seriously compete to establish signposts on such preferred stems at choice locations, wherein dominant individuals are likely to displace subordinates.

The typical scrape is not complete without a buck scent marking a slender, overhead branch.

Seeing that bucks responded so favorably to the aspen stems, I decided to conduct another short experiment using the same approach with hand-placed poles, to determine if bucks had a strong species preference for rubbing.

For my study, I chose four species that differed in bark toughness and aromatic quality: aspen, which was easily stripped and non-aromatic; black cherry, which was only slightly more difficult to strip and somewhat aromatic; balsam fir, which stripped quite easily and was highly resinous and aromatic; sugar maple, which was very difficult to debark and non-aromatic. All species were two inches in diameter, cut into eight-foot lengths and trimmed of branches, so that I essentially controlled for other stem physical features and for location.

Once again, I set my test rub poles along small openings. The four species were randomly positioned about 25 feet apart in a line to assure that all four species were offered in the same area at the same time and that a given stem's position relative to others was not important. I then checked each stem for signs of rubbing during a five-week period preceding and during the rut.

Of the four species tested, trembling aspen stems scored the highest; they were the most frequently rubbed (100 percent) and re-rubbed (96 percent), and showed the greatest average rub length (21 inches). Black cherry rated a respectable second place in all three categories (88 percent rubbed, 77 percent re-rubbed, and rubs averaging 15 inches long). Balsam fir and sugar maple were less frequently rubbed (60 percent and 44 percent, respectively) and seldom re-rubbed (20 percent and 9 percent, respectively). Average rub lengths on balsam fir (11 inches) and sugar maple (6.5 inches) were also less.

This brief experiment supported some previous study findings, challenged others, and demonstrated that bucks can be easily induced to make antler rubs when provided with the right kind of stem in the right location.

In my study, bucks showed a strong preference for trembling aspen. Although I did not test for size preferences, the high success I achieved with two-inch-diameter stems indicates that bucks must like them in that size range, which agrees with most other investigations. Also, as in the Maine studies, Northern Michigan bucks did not show a preference for rubbing trees that had aromatic qualities. Certainly, the fact that I used poles with good success also indicates that the rub stem's upper structure has little to do in determining desirable buck rubs.

Although I did not test for location, the exceptionally high rate of rubbing and re-rubbing success achieved in my experiments with poles positioned along forest

Studies indicate that some bucks return to a "traditional rub" year after year. This old rub has apparently received the attention of generations of deer.

openings, even with undesirable species like sugar maple, strongly suggests that openness and good visibility are key factors in determining signpost locations. Given my earlier experience with fake buck rubs, it's obvious that a deer can't really tell if a rub is authentic until the animal just about sticks its nose on one. Even then, some deer don't seem too sure.

Observations made by Leonard Rue III and Grant Woods suggest that certain types of buck rubs may serve special purposes. Rue has identified what he calls "licking sticks," which tend to be short, small-diameter, broken-off shrubs, whereas Woods has investigated "traditional rubs," which are large-diameter trees rubbed in successive years.

Most licking sticks I've encountered have been broken-off shrubs about three quarters of an inch in diameter and from two to three feet tall, and are usually located in open areas. They apparently originate when a buck vigorously rubs a slender stem until it snaps off at the point of heaviest rubbing. Rue reports that several different bucks may then subsequently visit, rub, and lick the same stem. Such a licking stick is only used for one season.

In South Carolina, Grant Woods found that bucks rubbed some of the same large trees year after year. He observed that older bucks, in particular, selected certain larger trees to rub, and re-rubbed the same tree frequently. Bucks he studied showed a strong preference for making traditional rubs on highly aromatic sassafras trees larger than three and a half inches in diameter.

Woods hypothesized that "...the aromatic qualities of sassafras must enhance its function as a source of olfactory communication by alerting deer in the area that a communication signpost is present. Once deer are alerted by the visual and aromatic qualities of a rubbed sassafras that a signpost is present, they can then approach the rub and receive or deliver an olfactory communication signal."

Studies conducted with tame free-ranging whitetails have shown that female deer are readily attracted to buck rubs less than two days old. While following tame deer, researchers found that adult does frequently paused and sniffed the exposed xylem of recently made buck rubs. The dominant doe, in particular, often licked or nibbled the rub and surrounding frayed bark, and sometimes even rubbed her forehead directly on the exposed xylem.

Using automatic cameras triggered by infrared sensors, Grant Woods photographed whitetails more that 300 times at or in the vicinity of traditional rubs on his South Carolina study area. Although more than half of the deer photographed were fawns, only one fawn was recorded investigating a rub. Does did not respond

Researchers have found that adult does often lick or nibble an exposed rub and frayed bark.

much better, as only three percent of them actually approached a rub for close inspection. By comparison, nearly 40 percent of the bucks Woods photographed were smelling, touching or rubbing a buck rub.

In a similar manner to Woods' investigation, I monitored artificially placed stems in the Cusino enclosure that had turned into "nontraditional rubs." Although about three quarters of the nearly 250 deer I photographed at rubbed poles were fawns and adult does, about 29 percent of each were recorded inspecting a rub. Adult bucks were less frequently photographed at rubs, but they were even more responsive. Nearly 60 percent of the yearlings and 40 percent of the older bucks photographed were either smelling or rubbing one of the poles.

I'm unable to explain why deer responded so differently to buck rubs in the two studies. It may be that the messages conveyed by bucks at rubs are highly variable and dependent upon whether a rub is traditional or not, its location, and probably many other factors we researchers have yet to identify. The observations strongly suggest, however, that dominant bucks are the primary message senders, whereas subordinates of both sexes are the primary message readers.

SCRAPES

The typical scrape is a round or, more commonly, oval-shaped area from two to three feet across where a whitetail buck has pawed away the surface duff to expose the soil and then urinated. A scent-marked, frayed branch nearly always extends above the pawed site. Since the full scrape-making sequence involves a combination of overhead branch marking, ground pawing, and urination, which are also employed independently for other reasons, whitetail scraping behavior represents a highly complex integration of various behaviors. Logically, therefore, the scrape probably conveys several different messages and likely serves multiple functions.

Studies conducted with captive deer in Georgia revealed that most scrapes are made by mature, dominant males. Subordinate males commonly inspected the pawed site and scent-marked the overhanging branch at a scrape, but they were never observed to paw or urinate at a scrape. Even in the absence of mature bucks, in my studies, yearling bucks only made about 15 percent as many scrapes as older bucks. The consensus among researchers, therefore, is that while scraping behavior among whitetail bucks is done instinctively, it is a trait that improves with practice and experience.

Although inconspicuous to the human eye, an annointed and scent-marked twig takes on magical attractive powers for both bucks and does that are still not fully understood.

It is believed that scraping is an instinctive behavior among whitetails, but one that improves with experience and practice.

Karl Miller proposes that scent-marking signals on the overhanging branch at a scrape convey buck identity and presence, whereas pawing of the ground denotes aggression by the dominant buck and his intent to forcefully exhibit his superior status if pushed to that extent. Urine deposited by the buck in the scrape, on the other hand, possibly relays information, to both bucks and does, regarding his social or physiological status, such as his dominance, health status or readiness to breed. Also, since scrapes are made primarily by dominant males, Miller suggests that females in estrus may seek scrapes in search of the best reproductive partner.

Although scraping behavior serves a very important, highly ritualized role during the whitetail's breeding season, bucks (and even does, occasionally) also sometimes scrape at other times of the year, especially during spring. This is another reason to suspect that whitetail communication via the scrape serves different purposes during different seasons.

Most researchers have focused their attention on determining the role that scent marking plays in the reproductive behavior of whitetails. In the process, they've solved many of the mysteries that formerly surrounded deer antler rubbing and scraping behavior. Only recently, however, have investigators attempted to describe the types and frequencies of scent marking employed by both sexes of deer throughout the year.

Larry Marchinton and other Georgia researchers were probably the first to document that whitetail bucks perform overhead branch marking as an important part of the full scrape-making sequence during autumn, but also separately at other times of the year. Their studies revealed that, unlike antler rubbing and ground pawing, bucks readily scent marked overhead branches year-round. Bucks of all social ranks reportedly marked branches and inspected those that had been marked by other bucks.

Marchinton suggested that overhead branch marking during the non-reproductive period communicates a buck's identity. He also noted that some, but not all, branches scent marked by bucks during the summer became active scrapes during autumn.

The limb above the well-pawed scrape is an intriguing structure. Sometimes it's a large, complex branch with many tips. Frequently, however, that special limb extending over the scrape consists only of one slender, quite inconspicuous, arching stem—looking somewhat like a bent fish pole—with a mutilated, pencil-thin tip. And yet, when that fragile twig is carefully manipulated and anointed by bucks, it takes on magical, attractive powers that are still not fully understood.

Apparently, most scrapes are made by mature, dominant males. Subordinate males may inspect a pawed sight and even scent mark the branch, but have not been observed pawing or scraping at another's scrape.

The overhead limb is the most important element of the scrape.
Remove the limb from a scrape and the scrape disappears. However,
adding a limb in the right location will draw bucks to form a new
scrape where none existed before.

Without the overhead limb there is no full-fledged scrape. If you take away the limb, the most traditional, diligently pawed scrape site will disappear. On the other hand, if you add a limb in the right location, bucks will paw the turf with dedication, forming a new scrape where none had ever existed.

Based upon tests conducted in the Cusino enclosure, I discovered that preferred scrape sites were those with concentrated deer activity, open understory vegetation, relatively level ground, and moderately dry, easily exposed soil. Furthermore, given the presence of mature bucks, I found that bucks could be easily induced to establish scrapes at such sites with reasonable regularity. All that was necessary was to provide a properly positioned, slender-bowed limb of five or six feet in length, so that the limb tip centered about five feet above a well traveled deer trail. Stems so positioned—slightly above head height on a buck—apparently served as a strong visual attraction for

scent marking by bucks; it seemed as though bucks could hardly resist marking them. Twenty-four of my first 40 test sites turned into buck scrapes within a five-week period.

In subsequent years, I positioned 50 pairs of these test limbs throughout the Cusino enclosure and used them to examine various aspects of deer scent-marking behavior. The advantage of my scheme, of course, was that I not only had very precise areas to inspect for pawing, but now I also had a large number of specific twigs to examine for evidence of scent marking.

In April 1988, I positioned one limb of each pair so that the tip of the limb centered about five feet over a deer trail, making it available to deer for marking. However, the companion limb at each site was left in an upright position until October, so that deer could not scent mark it prior to autumn. My objectives here were twofold: (1) I wanted to determine if my enclosure deer did indeed scent mark

The limb above the pawed scrape usually consists of a single, slender limb but is sometimes a large and complex branch.

The rub, scrape and scent-marked limb serve as extensions of the animal itself, announcing its presence and status to other deer.

during the summer months, and (2) I wanted to determine if prior scent marking played a major role in the establishment of scrapes during autumn.

Close inspection of those limbs made available for marking revealed that more than 90 percent of them were scent-marked by velvet-antlered bucks during spring and summer. I recorded an especially high frequency of scent marking during May and June, when the only evidence was deer hair found adhered to the limb tips.

It's interesting to note that I could detect no serious mutilation of the limb tips until bucks also started pawing the sites, usually during early October. During the non-reproductive period, deer (primarily bucks, as determined with automatic cameras) marked the limbs very gently, giving heavily used limb tips an oily or greased appearance. However, once bucks had shed their velvet and started pawing the scrapes, the limb tips above scraped sites often showed signs of being bitten, or many times of being broken off, probably due to vigorous thrashing of the limbs by the buck with its antlers. This would suggest that the manner in which bucks scent marked the limb tips changed seasonally. It also suggests that the substances being deposited and the messages being conveyed in such marking may differ throughout the year.

In my studies, more than 80 percent of the test limbs scent marked by deer prior to autumn turned into active scrapes, but so did about 60 percent of those not made available until autumn. Nonetheless, since bucks more frequently re-pawed sites that they had scent marked during the spring and summer, it seems as though prior scent communication plays some role in determining scrape site selection during autumn.

During 1991 and 1992, I used automatic cameras to record deer using the overhead limbs versus deer inspecting the pawed soil. Results of those photographic studies confirmed my prior suspicions and supported the findings reported by Marchinton, namely that the primary "markers" and "readers" involved in limb-marking behavior are bucks. Of 76 deer I photographed either marking or inspecting the overhead limbs, 65 were bucks, five were adult does, and six were fawns, despite an enclosure herd comprising roughly 30 percent bucks, 30 percent does and 40 percent fawns. By contrast, of nearly 200 deer photographed either pawing or inspecting the scrape, bucks, does and fawns were recorded in numbers proportionate to their occurrence in the population.

My observations are in general agreement with those of Marchinton, indicating that does and fawns do very little scent marking of overhead limbs or pawing of the ground at scrape sites. However, I did not expect to see such a strong sex difference with regard to inspection of the overhead limbs. If a doe visited an active scrape and smelled the urine-marked soil, I would have expected her to also smell the overhead limbs, which obviously was not always the case. Therefore, until I see strong evidence to the contrary, I'm inclined to believe that the messages attached to overhead limbs by whitetail bucks are primarily for the benefit of other bucks.

Most bucks I photographed were smelling the limb tip. However, some had their antlers or forehead up to the limb and others were obviously mouthing the tip or moving it along their snout. Most of the scent marking seemed to be by bucks three and a half years or older, especially during the breeding season, but even younger bucks marked limbs during the summer months.

To see a buck marking an overhead branch is some-

what like watching a baseball coach using coded sign language to signal a base runner—the many signals tend to include numerous false, meaningless gyrations that confuse all but the well-informed "reader." When marking overhead limbs, a buck may mouth the limb gently or chew it vigorously, rub it with his forehead, preorbital area, nose, chin or cheek, or thrash it with his antler. Even when in velvet, it's difficult to determine if the buck marks with his antlers or only his forehead. These same mysteries are readily evident in my photographic documentation of buck "limbing" behavior.

Secretions of likely importance in limb marking may come from the forehead glands, preorbital glands, nasal glands or saliva. Some investigators have even suggested that bucks might use their snout to transfer secretions deposited on their tarsal glands. It may well be that a number of glandular secretions are used in concert and that the use of any given secretion may vary seasonally.

When marking limbs, a buck may mouth the limb gently or chew it vigorously. He may caress it with his face or thrash it violently with his antler.

Nonetheless, given the seasonal differences we see in terms of limb use, the chemical ingredients used as signals and the messages they convey must change. I would be willing to speculate that glandular secretions from nasal glands or preorbital glands (or possibly from some yet unidentified source), in conjunction with saliva, play a highly important communal role among bucks year-round, whereas forehead glandular secretions, associated with aggression and antler thrashing of the limbs, become more important in conveying dominance status during the breeding season.

The individual deer's signposts serve as extensions of the animal itself. The rub, scrape, and scent-marked limbs serve as visual and olfactory reminders to other deer that "the maker is not here now, but was and will be later." During the non-breeding period, such "sign" left on overhead limbs may carry a rather congenial message: "If you'd like, leave a message and I'll get back to you as soon as possible." On the other hand, during the rut, that message may convey a totally different meaning, indicating that the "number one" buck is still alive, healthy, and ever present: "So beware! Heed my warning or be prepared to suffer the consequences."

Throughout the year, whitetail bucks of any social rank commonly scent mark overhead limbs and check those scent marked by others, but they seldom paw the ground at these sites except during the autumn rut period. Normally, on northern ranges, you will find minimal active scraping until the last week of September or, more commonly, the first week of October. As mentioned earlier, however, the timing of such activity will vary depending upon the age and experience of bucks in the area; bucks three and a half years of age or older will commence scraping in earnest three or more weeks earlier than younger bucks.

The best information available indicates that a buck's testosterone levels, his social position, his degree of physical maturity, and his behavioral maturity and rut experience interact to promote the expression of scraping behavior. However, there is also good evidence that even mature bucks may individually vary a great deal in their amount of scraping—some are avid scrape-makers, some are not. Also, competition appears to be an important factor causing excessive scraping wherever several mature, rut-experienced bucks work the same breeding range and compete for the attention of resident does.

All deer urinate onto their tarsal glands, which are located at the hock, on the inner surface of their hind legs, in a behavior referred to as rub-urination. When doing so, the animal crouches slightly, presses its hocks together, and then rubs its tarsal glands together while simultaneously urinating over them. Most deer normally lick off the excess urine that collects on their tarsal glands. During the primary breeding season, however, dominant bucks tend to rub-urinate much more frequently than usual, often in the soil of their scrapes, and seldom lick their tarsal glands.

The tarsal gland consists of a tuft of long hairs underlain by an area of enlarged sebaceous glands. The gland itself secretes a fatty substance that sticks to the specially shaped, long hairs associated with the gland. The musky odor that emanates from the tarsal area, especially of rutting bucks, however, is due to the urine that is deposited on the gland, not from the lipids themselves. As the urine flows over the tarsal hairs, the fatty material that was secreted from the glands onto the hairs selects out some molecules and holds them on the gland. Bacterial action of the urine trapped on the hairs, then, produces the rutting buck's characteristic musky odor.

Retaining the odor requires daily "recharging" of the gland with urine, in order for the buck to maintain its maximum effectiveness.

Karl Miller emphatically states: "…without a doubt, the tarsal gland is the most important gland to whitetails." I agree, as chemical signals emanating from the gland permit deer to recognize other deer and probably permit them to transfer a multitude of socially important information.

Miller notes that deer often sniff the tarsal glands of other deer. By doing so, he suggests, deer can not only tell who the other deer is, but can also determine the individual's sex, dominance status, and physical condition. Does apparently identify their fawns through the odors given off by fawns' tarsal glands, while bucks use this gland to advertise their dominance status and breeding condition, both to other bucks and to does.

Tarsal gland function is perhaps better understood

A buck "rub-urinating" across its tarsal glands and into its scrape. This possibly relays olfactory information regarding his social and physiological status to both other bucks and does.

than other chemical mechanism in whitetail communications. Although detailed chemical analysis of deer urine has not been completed, preliminary work has revealed considerable individual difference in its composition, in buck urine in particular. Certain compounds appear to be directly related to the male's age and dominance status, and are only found in the urine of dominant bucks during the breeding season. These differences could readily allow other deer, including estrous does, to identify a buck's dominance status and reproductive state, based upon urine odors deposited at scrapes.

Scraping activity generally peaks about two weeks before peak breeding, whereas deer visitations to scrapes peak concurrently with peak breeding. In the Upper Great Lakes region, we see a dramatic rise in the amount of scraping during late October and early November, about two weeks before peak breeding, but it decreases sharply thereafter. Given that this same pattern occurs annually, regardless of the age of bucks involved, it appears that certain factors strongly cued to changing photoperiod are responsible for causing a sudden increase in buck scraping behavior each autumn.

Other researchers have found that both black-tailed and white-tailed does exhibit a "silent" ovulation about two weeks before breeding, wherein females exhibit all the physiological signs of breeding, but not the psychological response. I've speculated that female pheromones associated with this silent ovulation function to stimulate and excite the males, thereby triggering their increase in scraping behavior a couple of weeks before breeding starts. If so, this would function as an adaptation to forewarn males of rapidly approaching breeding opportunities and help synchronize the breeding behavior of the sexes.

Highly controlled studies at the University of Georgia have revealed that in the presence of mature bucks, younger bucks do almost no scraping. Georgia biologists' findings suggest that odors produced by dominant bucks, in addition to the psychological stress involved, suppress the rutting behavior of subordinate males, and thereby help to maintain stable dominance hierarchies. Obviously, then, in the absence of domination, even younger bucks will demonstrate an elevation in testosterone secretion and scrape, albeit with far less intensity, due to their inexperience.

Few scrapes show repeated pawing for extended periods. Even those sites that are pawed repeatedly for five or six consecutive days are often ignored, for whatever reason, for days or weeks, only to show a resurgence of late-season use. On average, prime-age bucks only freshen and maintain slightly more than half of the scrapes they make, versus about a 40 percent retreatment rate for yearling bucks. Generally, due to their more frequent repawing of scrapes, prime-age bucks tend to make larger scrapes than do younger bucks.

Most studies have shown that scrapes are not randomly distributed. Instead, they tend to be clumped where the understory is relatively open and where concentrated deer activity occurs. Since scrapes presumably serve as an important means of communication between bucks and does during the breeding period, bucks usually position their scrapes where they get the most attention from does. Logically, those scrapes that receive little attention are soon abandoned.

Hunters sometimes make artificial, or "mock," scrapes in an attempt to entice deer and improve their chances for hunting success. I've also experimented with mock scrapes, using my test-limb sites, wherein I've cleared away the surface duff to mimic a buck's pawing, applied urine collected from rutting bucks to the exposed soil, then monitored and compared deer response to treated versus non-treated sites.

I found that deer were readily attracted to the artificial scrapes I produced, but that bucks responded rather erratically. Given a choice to paw my mock scrapes or make their own scrape beneath a nearby limb, however, bucks more readily developed their own new scrapes rather than take over those I had made. Furthermore, although bucks sometimes pawed my fake scrapes, they often pawed their own circular or oval area beside mine rather than enlarge the one I had made.

Although bucks frequently visit scrapes made by other bucks, and two or more bucks may occasionally compete to dominate the same scraped site, I'm convinced that individual bucks are more inclined to make and maintain their own exclusive scrapes. These observations lead me to believe that a buck's scrapes are pretty much his personal property.

While whitetail bucks are not truly territorial, the research conducted by Gerald Moore and Larry Marchinton suggests that a buck's scrapes serve as dominance areas, or his "mini-breeding territories," because he sometimes defends his scrapes from use by other bucks and he seems to enjoy a higher dominance rank in the vicinity of his scrapes then he might elsewhere. Therefore, within a buck's breeding range are interspersed many small, strongly defended intolerance zones immediately around his scrapes. Some evidence indicates that subordinate bucks sometimes behave cautiously while in the vicinity of a dominant buck's scrapes or that they may avoid these sites altogether.

The maker of a rub may often pause to inspect his progress, smelling
and licking at intervals.

The rub, scrape and scent-marked limbs are reminders to other deer that, "The maker is not here now, but was and will be later!"

However, contradictory evidence gathered through the use of automatic cameras indicates that bucks of any social rank may inspect the scent-marked limbs and pawed scrape sites of dominant bucks.

There is plenty of evidence to indicate that adult does and fawns show interest in scrapes and are, in fact, attracted to them. Moore and Marchinton reported that does commonly approached scrapes and urinated in them, and left a strong scent trail leading away from the scrape. Upon returning to check his scrape, then, the buck was observed to make grunting sounds as he encountered the doe's scent trail and move off at a fast walk with his nose to the ground. The buck generally found the doe easily, within two hundred yards of the scrape. In most cases, the investigators noted, the buck and doe associated only briefly. However, if the doe was nearing estrus, the buck stayed with her, often trotting or running after her until she would stand for mounting. Moore and Marchinton reported: "One such 'chase' continued for three days. Copulation was observed twice on the third day at a location 1.1 miles from the scrape where the doe's trail was initially encountered."

While following tame deer, Timothy Sawyer found that does appeared to encounter scrapes by chance. Upon finding a scrape, however, the does frequently stopped to sniff the scrape, walked through it, or occasionally urinated near it.

Considering the apparent personal nature of scrapes, and the fact that bucks tend to position their scrapes where does are most likely to encounter them, the question then arises: Do female whitetails demonstrate mate selection by selectively visiting the scrapes made by males they prefer as mates, deposit chemical signals at those scrapes, and thereby solicit the attention of certain bucks to father their young? In theory, the doe that "chooses" to mate with a large-bodied, large-antlered buck is selecting an individual possessing superior hereditary traits, thus assuring thrifty progeny and the perpetuation of genetic fitness within the herd.

To date, that question remains essentially unanswered. Obviously, however, in order for such a selective process to operate, the sexes must be able to communicate their identity and reproductive state. Also, in order for the female to be truly mate-selective, she must be able to relate specific male odors detected at the buck's signposts to the individual buck himself. Given what we researchers know about the subject, whitetails seem well endowed with an elaborate lexicon of "chemical language" and appear quite capable of communicating such information through glandular secretions, urine deposits, saliva, and probably other sources.

If female whitetails do demonstrate some form of mate selection, then it seems that the scrape might be a good place for the transfer of such information between the sexes. However, if such female mate selection is operative in whitetails, and if it does occur at the scrape, it must be almost totally restricted to those populations that harbor older, rut-experienced bucks, because younger bucks make relatively few scrapes and instead employ more of a seek-and-chase-style courtship.

COURTSHIP AND BREEDING

T he general timing of the whitetail's breeding season is set by changing photoperiod—the shortening days in autumn— but numerous environmental, biological and behavioral factors may interact to determine when, or even if, an individual doe may breed. As a result, whitetail breeding schedules tend to vary considerably throughout the species' range, and sometimes even from one year to the next within the same area, depending upon many natural and man-induced circumstances.

Generally, the breeding season is quite brief in the North, where it is also rather tightly regulated by photoperiod. In the South, however, factors other than day length also become highly important and often contribute to long breeding seasons.

Physiologically, adult whitetail bucks are ready to breed long before the females. Except during estrus, does avoid the constant attentions of bucks checking for breeding receptiveness.

In regions with severe winter weather, it is absolutely essential that does are bred during a limited period of time, for their fawns to be born on schedule in spring, when weather and food conditions are most favorable for the newborn's survival. Also, the young animal must have ample time, as well as excellent nutrition, in order to achieve its maximum growth potential prior to facing its first stressful winter season. Such tightly controlled breeding schedules tend to be inherited; those renegade mothers that attempt to breed at any other than the most optimal time produce few, or no, surviving offspring to perpetuate such an undesirable trait.

In the Great Lakes Region, as is probably true throughout the whitetail's northern range, the rut may span three to four months, sometimes starting in late September and occasionally extending through January, but that's about the maximum seasonal range. More commonly, the northern whitetail rut will be quite brief and very intense. The first does usually breed during the latter part of October, but about 80 to 90 percent of the adult does will breed during November, with peak breeding occurring around mid-month. Young females, those less than 18 months of age, will represent most of the late-breeders, who conceive in late November, December, or possibly even January.

In the South, however, where the winter season is not normally so stressful, both unusually early-born and late-born fawns may survive and eventually reproduce. There the timing and duration of the breeding period is potentially more variable, often leading to unusually protracted breeding seasons extending into February or even March.

In Mississippi, for example, breeding may span four or five months, with peak breeding activity occurring between mid-December and mid-January, as it does in South Texas. Likewise, in the flatwood habitats of northwestern Florida, investigator Steve Shea found that most does did not breed until January or February, thus giving birth to fawns during August or September.

Physiologically, compared to females, adult whitetail bucks are more advanced and ready to breed long before the females are receptive. It is generally assumed that adult bucks are capable of breeding while carrying mature, velvet-free antlers. If so, then in Upper Michigan, prime-age bucks are ready to breed nearly two months before the first does normally become receptive. Even in states like Mississippi, adult bucks generally shed velvet during September, but most does do not breed until nearly three months later.

Some of these late-breeding, late-birthing schedules, which are common in many southern herds, are due to nutritional shortages and resultant retarded growth rates among deer. But, as alluded to earlier, other delayed breeding schedules appear to be the direct result of a shortage of mature bucks and tend to be hunting induced. Therefore, late breeding schedules may sometimes be advanced, and made more synchronous, by changing the deer harvest regulations to more carefully balance deer numbers with available food and cover resources and to permit more males to survive to maturity.

By the time the first does come into estrus, mature bucks will have formed a strict dominance hierarchy that minimizes fighting competition for mating privileges. Therefore, even if estrous females do not demonstrate mate selection via communication through odors at the scrape, as suggested earlier, the dominance hierarchy ensures that the most physically-fit males will do most of the breeding—as long as older males exist within the population.

Even in socially disrupted populations (those lacking a strict dominance hierarchy among males) where all sires are of yearling age, some degree of mate selection will occur, because females tend to avoid the sexual advances of young, related, reproductively active males. This too can be viewed as a form of mate selection because moving away from a suitor, or rejecting him, can be instrumental in determining with whom a doe will mate.

Except during estrus, does normally avoid bucks. However, I've witnessed different patterns of avoidance by females in response to the sexual advances of males that, to me, suggest does may sometimes give favorable, and other times unfavorable, visual signals to the buck. For example, in some instances a female might flee even at the distant sight of a particular buck. At other times, however, she might run a tight circle around him or run back and forth in front of the buck before leaving the scene. Although both scenarios demonstrate avoidance, they seem to convey different messages. What the doe may be communicating could vary with her physiological state, relative to her pending estrus, as well as the particular male involved.

About the time bucks become solitary travelers and scraping activity escalates, they start to chase does in earnest, testing them for breeding receptiveness. This sudden change in behavior, which occurs only a few weeks before the first females breed, is probably triggered by increased production of testosterone in males, in addition to seasonal changes in female scent and behavior.

Once bucks exhibit this behavioral change, they become extremely active and travel from one doe group to the next, searching for estrous females. The mature buck in rut rests only briefly, as he travels day and night,

Once a buck locates a doe in estrus that is willing to stand for copulation, he stays close, tending her carefully and driving off other bucks attracted by the sex pheromones emitted by the doe.

Older bucks will court females with much more finesse than less experienced young bucks. Rutting behavior may be largely instinctive but, like scraping, experience and learninq serve to sharpen and fine-tune courtship skills.

feeds very little, and loses 20 to 25 percent of his body weight within a four- to five-week period.

We know now that the whitetail rut includes a timely sequence of complex ecological, physiological, and behavioral events that commence weeks before the first doe breeds. Restricted food sources, gathering of the female clans, dispersal of young males, formation of strict dominance hierarchies, and extensive signposting by dominant bucks characterize that period we commonly refer to as pre-rut. And although the whitetail buck's rutting behavior is largely instinctive, learning and experience serve to sharpen and finely tune the courtship skills of those that will most likely sire the next generation. Older, more behaviorally mature bucks will court females, soliciting their attention and testing their receptivity, with much more finesse than young bucks that are rut inexperienced.

While overly energetic yearling bucks may wildly chase does once visual contact with them is made, older bucks experienced in courtship and breeding are more inclined to test the receptivity of does in a highly ritualized fashion. The prime-age buck will trot in short, choppy steps toward the doe, holding his neck outstretched and his head low to the ground while keeping his muzzle slightly elevated. He may simultaneously grunt or emit a snort or wheeze-snort as he exhales through his flared nostrils. The apparent purpose of such behavior is to encourage the female to urinate so that the buck can then determine, through the detection of certain odors associated with the doe's urine, if she is approaching estrus. The doe's urine, then, becomes a precious commodity to her during the rut; it not only allows her to signal her willingness to breed, it also permits her to leave negative messages, thus saving her from being relentlessly pursued at other times.

The doe obviously informs the buck that she is in estrus and ready to breed through chemical signals, or pheromones, often, but not always, deposited in her urine. The rut-experienced buck will sniff the doe's urine or taste it immediately after he sees her urinate, and within a few seconds will be able to determine whether the doe is approaching estrus.

But just how the buck makes that determination is still not perfectly clear to researchers. Obviously, it involves chemical signals, of which there are three basic types: (1) releaser pheromones, which evoke an immediate behavioral response, (2) priming pheromones, which result in a physiological response, and (3) informer pheromones, which relay information but generally do not result in a behavioral or physiological response. This same reasoning can be applied to the messages contained in doe urine.

There are two avenues by which the buck can receive chemical signals deposited in doe urine: One pathway is through the nose and main olfactory system, the other is by way of what is referred to as the vomeronasal organ. It appears that these two systems serve different behavioral and physiological functions.

Odor detection through the main olfactory system is accomplished by receiving airborne chemicals through the nose. Nerve fibers located in the olfactory epithelium of the nose carry the sensation of smell along the olfactory nerve to olfactory lobe of the brain. The odor information is then transmitter to various parts of the brain and processed. Logically, then, if the chemical signals included releaser pheromones that signal a doe's estrus condition, the process would evoke a mating pursuit response by the buck.

The vomeronasal seems to serve an entirely different function. Examining the roof of a deer's mouth, one will see a small opening near the center. This is the opening of the vomeronasal organ, which apparently is employed to analyze deer urine. In this case, the buck will not only sniff the doe's urine, he will taste it, oftentimes performing a lip-curl, or "flehmen." In doing so, he holds his neck and chin upward at about a 45-degree angle, opens his mouth slightly, curls his upper lip, and closes his nostrils. According to Karl Miller and Larry Marchinton: "...this pumps some urine into the vomeronasal organ for analysis."

However, chemical signals obtained through the vomeronasal organ do not follow nerve pathways to the same parts of brain as those that enter through the nose. Instead, Miller and Marchinton emphasize that "...nerves from the vomeronasal organ travel through the accessory olfactory system, in which nerves are connected via a single synapse in the accessory olfactory bulb to a part of the brain called the amygdala, which in turn has direct connections to the hypothalamus. This is important, since the hypothalamus is the part of the brain that controls the reproductive physiology of the deer through the production of hormones."

In other words, priming pheromones received from the doe's urine likely pass through the vomeronasal system and have a direct effect upon the buck's reproductive physiology, but probably do not evoke an immediate behavioral response as in the case of releaser pheromones. This essentially suggests that the buck does not use the flehmen response to determine if a doe is in estrus.

Another major difference between the nose and vomeronasal systems, as pointed out by Miller and Marchinton "...is that the main olfactory (nose) system appears to be used to analyze smaller, more volatile,

A rut-experienced buck will approach does in a highly ritualized fashion, trotting in short, choppy steps with head low and neck outstretched.

Whitetail bucks use their noses to detect "releaser pheromones."

airborne molecules, and the vomeronasal system to analyze larger, less volatile molecules that are in solution in some liquid, such as urine."

Although no direct experimentation has been done with white-tailed deer, the University of Georgia researchers (citing extensive studies done with sheep and goats) suggest that whitetail bucks use both systems (nose and vomeronasal) to good advantage during the rut. They propose that the vomeronasal system is used to determine whether the doe is *approaching* estrus, whereas bucks use their nose to detect volatile chemical compounds indicating that a doe is *in* estrus.

Given the above considerations, one might expect bucks to demonstrate the flehmen response more frequently just prior to the primary breeding season, and more often toward does not yet in estrus. Observational studies generally confirm those expectations. In addition, since the vomeronasal system is connected to that part of the brain that controls the buck's reproductive physiology, Miller and Marchinton believe that "...a male's analysis of (a doe's) urine through this system likely serves to prime that physiology and thereby ensure that he reaches peak reproductive condition at the same time as do the females."

If the predictions made by Miller and Marchinton prove correct, then both bucks and does employ the vomeronasal system to ensure reproductive synchrony. Females likely receive the all important priming pheromones from glandular secretions and urine deposited by bucks at their rubs and scrapes, whereas bucks receive the critical messages through analysis of doe urine, after inducing them to urinate by employing their ritualized mating approach.

Bucks actually detect a doe's estrus condition by inhaling fumes containing releaser pheromones. But those special odors do not come directly from the doe's urine, as one might expect.

During preliminary trials conducted at the University of Georgia, researchers tested the response of deer to urine collected directly from the bladders of does known to be in estrus with that of non-estrus urine, buck urine, and several control solutions, including salt water. Their experimental design consisted of using automatic aerosol dispensers to release test materials about every 15 minutes into circular areas of lightly tilled soil about three feet in diameter. Then they tallied the number of deer tracks at each site, after 24, 48, and 72 hours, to see if deer were more readily attracted to any of the test solutions.

Results of their study revealed that deer visited about one-fourth of the test sites each day, but the investigators could detect no preference for any of the solutions used.

That is, deer came to the salt water just about as readily as they did to the bonafide doe-in-heat urine. They concluded, therefore, that urine collected directly from the bladder of estrous does did not contain those potent releaser pheromones as most deer biologists would have predicted.

In another study, student Mark Whitney, under the guidance of Miller and Marchinton, conducted a rather involved series of trials with penned deer, wherein bucks were introduced to does artificially treated with estrous urine, non-estrous urine, estrous vaginal secretions, and water. Although individual responses varied, bucks devoted significantly more attention to the does treated with estrous vaginal secretions.

These experiments produced rather convincing evidence that it is not the urinary tract but the female reproductive tract, and associated vaginal secretions during the time of estrus, that is the primary source of pheromones that serve as sexual attractants.

These findings were confirmed by the Georgia researchers in subsequent studies.

Given that the releaser pheromones signalling a doe's estrus condition are in her vaginal secretions, then, the doe does not necessarily have to urinate in order to signal a buck of her receptiveness. All that is really necessary is that the buck be able to approach the doe close enough to smell her urogenital area.

During most of the year, female whitetails show a strong avoidance for adult males; does rarely let males approach closely until they are nearing estrus. Aside from very subtle posturing differences associated with estrus, researchers have been unable to identify any special pre-estrus visual warnings given by the female to the male that indicates her ensuing willingness to breed. Nor is there any evidence that she vocalizes to announce her estrus condition. Once the buck can approach the doe close enough to smell and lick her urogenital area and tarsal glands,

Bucks receive critical scent messages regarding breeding receptivity via the doe's urine after inducing her to urinate.

Once the buck can approach the doe close enough to smell and lick her urogenital area and tarsal glands, it is likely she is approaching a receptive stage.

however, he has some hint that she is at least approaching a receptive stage. Since bucks seem to be able to detect a doe's approaching estrus at least several hours, if not days, before she will accept copulation, the experienced buck will generally follow behind the doe at a reasonable distance until she is receptive. Sometimes, several bucks may follow along in single file, the most dominant being first in line.

While monitoring the activity patterns of penned does at the Cusino Wildlife Research Station, we found that, in the absence of a tending buck, the doe shows a dramatic rise in her nighttime movement activity (about 28 times normal) one to two nights before estrus. This restlessness is coincident with increased ovarian production of estrogen, the female hormone that precipitates a doe's mating urge. In one instance we calculated that a penned doe walked over 20 miles the night prior to mating. At the time, we speculated that such extensive wanderings would be adaptive in that they'd increase a doe's chances of finding a mate if one were not already in close attendance.

Later, while monitoring the activities of radio-collared deer at the National Zoo's Conservation and Research Center at Front Royal, Virginia, Stefan Holzenbein and Georg Schwede tested the presumption that free-ranging female whitetails might search for mates during their brief period of estrus. Instead, these researchers discovered that seven of eight females they followed restricted their movements to core areas of their home range around the time of estrus. There the does were presumably located by bucks and bred. But one doe suddenly started wandering and left her home range shortly before her estrus, apparently because she had not been located by a potential mate.

Holzenbein and Schwede concluded that female whitetails usually make their location predictable by restricting their movements before they become receptive, making it relatively easy for the buck to find them. Such a concentration of female activity likely accounts for a buck's tendency to cluster his scrapes in certain locations, namely where he might attract the greatest attention from prospective mates. However, if a doe attains estrus without being found by a buck, she might wander extensively and search for a mate.

A doe will only accept a male during peak estrus, which lasts for about 24 to 36 hours. If she is not bred, or for some reason does not become pregnant, the cycle may recur in 23 to 30 days. Thereafter, if she remains in peak physical condition but does not become pregnant, she might, on northern ranges, recycle for the third time. In milder southern climates, however, an unbred adult doe might come into estrus as many as seven times during one season. This considerable difference from north to south in the number of times a doe might come into estrus during a single season is another reason for potentially protracted whitetail breeding seasons in the South.

Once a buck locates a doe in estrus that is willing to stand for copulation, he stays close and carefully tends her. He'll drive away all other deer, including the doe's fawns of the previous spring, but especially other bucks that also are readily attracted by the sex pheromones emitted by the estrous doe. This pair-bond breeding system, which normally occurs among forest-dwelling whitetails, differs considerably from that of deer inhabiting the open savanna grasslands of Texas, where bucks show a tendency toward a harem-type breeding behavior, wherein each dominant buck attempts to control a group of does.

The breeding pair may mate several times during their bonding period and might stay together from 24 to 72 hours. The available evidence suggests that the buck is capable of only one or two fertile ejaculations daily, and that mating may occur at any time during the day or night.

Some researchers suggest that estrus among all but the youngest of related reproducing females should be synchronous, because estrus can be induced by male-produced pheromones. Therefore, if a dominant female and a subordinate female come into estrus at the same time, the dominant doe might displace the subordinate and copulate first. If so, subordinate does are more likely to delay mating or will more readily mate with a subordinate male. On the other hand, if adult females of a clan come into estrus only a few days apart, a dominant buck might remain with the clan for several days and breed several does within a relatively short period of time.

Subtle social factors relative to a doe's societal standing within a matriarchal unit, as well as social stress due to crowding at high deer density, can influence a doe's rate of physical maturation and be extremely important in determining her reproductive performance. Certainly it "costs" the matriarch, in terms of energy expenditure, to maintain her dominance, but the exact costs and benefits incurred are poorly understood.

While some researchers speculate that the cost of maintaining dominance is greater than that required for subordinance, others provide evidence that the physiological consequences of subordination include reduced reproductive success, thus seeming to indicate that subordination is even more expensive. Most likely, the selective advantages of aggression and the attainment of dominance change according to the availability of food and cover resources.

The breeding pair may mate several times during a bonding period of one to three days.

Maternal success largely governs a doe's rate of behavioral maturity and will have considerable impact upon her reproductive performance.

Generally, older, maternally experienced does within a clan are most dominant; they also tend to control the most favorable habitat and maintain the best physical condition. As a result, prime-age matriarchs tend to breed first, conceive multiple litters, and produce disproportionately more female offspring. Obviously, the only way a doe can become a matriarch is to produce surviving daughters.

By contrast, subordination tends to have a strong suppressor-effect on a doe's reproductive performance. Young subordinate does breeding for their first time (fawns, yearlings, or sometimes two-and-a-half-year-olds) not only mate later, they also more commonly conceive single fetuses and a higher percentage of males. Even three-year-old does that fail to raise fawns often revert to subordinate female behavior by seeking close association

with their mother, and they exhibit reproductive traits comparable to younger does. Such effects, associated with poor maternal success, especially among first- and second-time mothers, become most pronounced at high herd density, sometimes even when deer are adequately nourished.

While conducting controlled breeding trials at the Cusino Wildlife Research Station, we found that adult does suffering poor nutrition prior to breeding not only bred late and conceived fewer progeny when compared with mothers on a good diet, but malnourished does also produced a higher than normal proportion of male fawns.

Surprisingly, however, we also observed that the timing of a doe's mating relative to her onset of estrus influenced the sex of her progeny. Does that bred comparatively late in estrus (from 49 to 95 hours) produced a preponderance (81 percent) of males. First-time breeders, in particular, seemed quite apprehensive

A bonded pair of whitetails at rest, the alert buck in close attendance. Such pair-bonding is typical of forest-dwelling whitetails. Harem-type breeding behavior is usually associated with deer of the open grasslands.

about breeding, usually did not mate until late in their cycle, and produced an excess of males. By comparison, does bred early in estrus (from 13 to 24 hours), most commonly maternally-experienced prime-aged does, conceived relatively few (14 percent) males.

How deer adjust, biologically, to alter their time of breeding and achieve a sex-selective breeding strategy is unknown. However, assuming that psychological stress is accompanied by certain hormonal imbalances, then the physiological consequences associated with subordination may function to inhibit, or at least alter, a doe's reproductive traits.

From our studies, for example, we learned that the adrenal gland can secrete significant amounts of progesterone, especially among stressed animals, and that abnormally high progesterone levels could block other hormonal effects necessary for ovulation. The overall effects of social stress, therefore, could account for a delay in ovulation or else delay a

submissive doe's receptivity, thus contributing to some potentially interesting reproductive spin-offs.

The whitetail's ability to vary the time that it breeds and the number and sex of the progeny it conceives represent far more than mere biological curiosities. Such reproductive adjustments probably evolved as a means of maximizing an individual doe's fawn-rearing success according to her prevailing social environment and the availability of forage resources. Therefore, a general assessment of the whitetail's breeding performance in any given area will provide considerable insight into the social and nutritional well-being of the local deer population.

Noted scientist Tony Peterle suggests that in their evolution deer should have developed certain socio-biological traits that would function to control population growth in the face of constantly fluctuating, "patchy" food resources, as likely occurred during pristine times. Along with reduced productivity when maternal

Older, more maternally-experienced does within a clan are usually the most dominant, tending to control the best habitat, breeding first and conceiving multiple litters.

nutrition is poor, the concomitant and disproportionate production of male fawns (which would likely disperse from the mother's area) would help slow the local population's growth. Conversely, when forage availability increased, it would then benefit the doe to produce an excess of daughters, because this would allow a clan to gain control over a favorable patch of habitat in the most socially compatible manner possible, and magnify the matriarch's genetic contribution to rapidly increasing numbers of deer.

Dale McCullough also argues that sometimes there are distinct benefits associated with producing male progeny—especially large, healthy ones—when the habitat is not conducive for population growth. Given limited resources, it would behoove a doe to produce only one fawn, preferably a son, annually. Since males normally disperse from their natal range, a son reared by a doe in poor habitat might more likely find favorable habitat elsewhere, while relieving his mother of added competition for limited resources. Furthermore, should food supplies improve at some future date, a healthy son might someday become a dominant buck and sire many offspring, thereby increasing the probability of passing on maternal genes.

On northern range, the whitetail's breeding season might terminate abruptly with the sudden onset of cold, wintery weather. Low temperatures and snow cover will force deer to shift from feeding on nutritious autumn forage to eating less-nourishing, woody browse. This combination of low-quality diet and accelerated body heat loss will force deer into a negative energy balance, meaning that more calories must be burned for basic body needs than are assimilated from the food the deer consume. This abrupt switch in metabolism, which may occur as early as late November or as late as early January in the Upper Great Lakes region, can interrupt breeding, especially among doe fawns, and even interrupt breeding among adult does during years when blizzard-like conditions strike earlier than usual.

In the North, cold weather and heavy snowfall may trigger deer migrations to wintering habitat especially early, sometimes even during the height of the November rut. But if weather should moderate, deer may return to their summer ranges within a few days. Radio-tracking studies conducted by Mike Nelson and Dave Mech in Northeastern Minnesota indicate deer sometimes make several treks between summer and winter range during late autumn before settling in preferred habitat for the duration of winter.

Low temperatures tend to be the primary stimulus prompting deer to migrate from summer to winter range during late autumn or early winter, but the animal's level

A matriarch doe may produce disproportionately more female offspring to add to her clan.

of nutrition also seems to be important. The work by Nelson and Mech revealed that some deer migrated much earlier than others, presumably because deer differed in their physiological thresholds to temperature and responded accordingly. These investigators suggest that whitetails on good diet may be more tolerant of cold temperatures and therefore migrate later than poorly nourished animals that are more sensitive to cold weather. (A similar relationship has been reported for black bears, wherein well-fed bears attain dormancy later than poorly fed ones.)

The whitetail's breeding season in the Midwest farmbelt is usually prolonged, sometimes ending in February, due primarily to the large number of doe fawns achieving puberty and breeding when six to seven months old. Unlike in northern forested areas, where most doe fawns fail to attain the threshold fat/lean body mass ratio necessary to achieve puberty, deer living on the fertile farmlands of the Midwest enjoy milder climate, excellent year-round nutrition, and live at lower densities with less social stress. The superb living conditions permit both sexes to exhibit an advanced rate of physical and behavioral maturity. More than 70 percent of doe fawns commonly breed in the intensively farmed lands of Illinois, Ohio, Indiana and Iowa, thus prolonging the breeding season and adding a totally new dimension to the whitetail's autumn behavior in that region.

Since whitetail does living in the farm country of the Midwest are extremely successful in rearing their fawns, even young does generate a family of their own and become matriarchs at a relatively young age. As a result, the breeding performance of a one-and-a-half-year-old farmland doe is more like that of a two-and-a-half-year-old doe living in northern forested habitat; the maternally experienced yearling tends to breed early in the rut, more likely conceives twins or triplets, and tends to produce an excess of female offspring.

Given that female fawns achieve puberty when conditions are favorable, there's a good chance that some male fawns also become sexually active under the right circumstances, especially as prevail in rich farmland. There is ample evidence, based upon studies of penned deer and field observations of wild deer, that well-nourished six- to seven-month-old males are capable of breeding.

What role buck fawns might play, if any, in the whitetail's breeding season is unknown. Normally, the domination by older bucks would prevent buck fawns from mating. In the Midwest, however, older bucks tend to be heavily exploited by hunting during November, yet thousands of doe fawns breed during December and January. In such cases, one must wonder if buck fawns play a significant role in breeding during late stages of the rut.

Throughout the South, the length of the whitetail's breeding season tends to be highly variable, but often prolonged, for different reasons. There, many young, late-born female whitetails do not achieve sexual maturity and breed until late in the rut, whereas many adult does exhibit estrus re-cycling and late-season breeding because they are not bred during their first estrus cycles.

Mississippi State University researcher Harry Jacobson notes that delayed breeding among whitetails has become even more pronounced in north-central Mississippi since the late 1960s. He raises an important question: "Do such does continue to breed late in subsequent years; and if so, how is their fecundity affected?" Jacobson blames much of the late-breeding upon the scarcity of adult bucks. He recommends delaying the buck hunting harvest until mid-December, thereby creating more of a balanced sex ratio among adult deer during the peak of the rut, and increasing the probability that does are bred during their first estrus.

Whitetail bucks will remain in rutting condition, fasting and expending enormous amounts of energy, as long as there are does to be bred. Therefore, the prolonged, highly enervating rut may produce several potentially devastating effects.

Typically, late breeding produces fawns that are abnormally small, unthrifty, and highly vulnerable when they face their first winter. Given poor to mediocre food conditions, the survivors may never achieve their maximum growth potential and ultimately will grow up to be stunted adults. The prolonged rut also leaves adult bucks terribly debilitated, with little time to recover sufficiently before facing the nutritional hardships normally associated with the winter season. If especially severe winter conditions should bring undue nutritional shortage on the heals of consecutive, prolonged rutting seasons, lean breeder bucks and small stunted fawns will be ill-prepared for survival. Many of those with meager energy reserves will likely succumb to malnutrition and predation during winter.

While the autumn season may linger in the South, it sometimes ends with brutal suddenness in the North. Regardless, eventually, the overpowering effects of chang-ing photoperiod will trigger physiological changes in deer that alter their behavior and closes the whitetail breeding window.

Whitetails will become more energy conservative and adopt a slower-paced lifestyle in the months ahead—they must if they are to survive. But with autumn's end, seeds of the next generation will have been planted. And, prepared or not, whitetails will face a another stressful winter season, one that may be far more perilous in some regions of the country than in others.

How well whitetails fare in the critical months ahead, and how well future generations of them fare, will hinge heavily upon environmental pressures and the availability of food and cover resources during the winter season. But the stage will already have been set; what had transpired during those previous intriguing couple of months—whitetail autumn—will have a strong bearing upon the outcome.

Testing the wind for signs of a breeding doe, this whitetail buck performs a lip-curl, or "flehmen."

The prolonged rut leaves adult bucks terribly debilitated with little time to recover before the onslaught of winter. Many bucks, weakened by the peak activity of the season, will succumb to malnutrition or predation in the weeks and months ahead.

SELECTED REFERENCES

Atkeson, T. D., and R. L. Marchinton. 1982. Forehead glands in white-tailed deer. *J. Mammal.* 63:613-617.

Atkeson, T. D., V. F. Nettles, R. L. Marchinton and W. V. Branan. 1988. Nasal glands in the Cervidae. *J. Mammal.* 69:153 156.

Benner, J. M., and R. T. Bowyer. 1988. Selection of trees for rubs by white-tailed deer in Maine. *J. Mammal.* 69:624-627

Brown, B. A. 1974. Social organization in male groups of white tailed deer. Pages 436-446 in V. Geist and F. Walther, eds. *The behavior of ungulates and its relation to management.* Int. Union Conserv. Na. Pub. 24, Morges, Switzerland. IUCN 940 pp.

Brown, R. D., ed. 1988. Antler development in Cervidae. Caesar Kleberg Wildl. Res. Inst., Kingsville, TX. 480 pp.

Bubenik, A. B. l972. North American moose management in light of European experiences. Kingsville, TX. 480 pp.

Cheatum, E. L., and G. H. Morton. 1946. Breeding seasons of white-tailed deer in New York. *J. Wildl. Manage.* 10:249-263.

Cox, D. J., and J. J. Ozoga. 1988. *Whitetail Country.* Willow Creek Press, Wautoma, WI. 145 pp.

de Vos, A. 1967. Rubbing of conifers by white-tailed deer in successive years. *J. Mammal.* 48:146-147

Follman, E. H., and W. D. Klimstra. 1969. Fertility in male white-tailed deer fawns. *J. Wildl. Manage.* 33:708-711.

Geist, V. 1981. Behavior: adaptive strategies in mule deer. Pp. 157-223, in O. C. Wallmo, ed. *Mule and black-tailed deer in North America.* University of Nebraska Press, Lincoln. 624 pp.

Gurver, B. J., D. C. Guynn, Jr. and H. A. Jacobson. 1984. Simulated effects of harvest strategy on reproduction in white-tailed deer. *J. Wildl. Manage.* 48:535-541.

Guynn, D. C., J. R. Sweeney, R. J. Hamilton and R. L. Marchinton. 1988. A case study in quality deer management. Pages 72-79 in R. J. Hamilton, ed. Proc. White-tailed Deer Manage. Seminar., Fort Jackson, S.C.

Halls, L. K., ed. 1984. *White-tailed deer: ecology and management.* Wildl. Manage. Inst., The Stackpole Co., Harrisburg, PA. 870 pp.

Hawkins, R. E., and W. D. Klimstra. 1970. A preliminary study of the social organization of white-tailed deer. *J. Wildl. Manage.* 34:407-419.

Hawkins, R. E., W. D. Klimstra and D. C. Autry. 1971. Dispersal of deer from Crab Orchard National Wildlife Refuge. *J. Wildl. Manage.* 35:216-220.

Hirth, D. H. 1977. Social behavior of white-tailed deer in relation to habitat. Wildl. Monogr. 53. 55 pp.

Holzenbein, S., and R. L. Marchinton. 1992. Emigration and mortality in orphaned male white-tailed deer. *J. Wildl. Manage.* 56:147-153.

Holzenbein, S., and G. Schwede. l989. Activity and movements of female white-tailed deer during the rut. *J. Wildl. Manage.* 53:219-223.

Hoskinson, R. L., and L. D. Mech. 1976. White-tailed deer migration and its role in wolf predation. *J. Wildl. Manage.* 40:439-441.

Kile, T. L., and R. L. Marchinton. 1977. White-tailed deer rubs and scrapes: spatial, temporal and physical characteristics and social role. Am. Midl. Nat. 97:257-266.

Knox, W. M., K. V. Miller, D. C. Collins, P. B. Bush, T. E. Kiser and R. L. Marchinton. 1992. Serum and urinary levels of reproductive hormones associated with the estrous cycle in white-tailed deer (*Odocoileus virginianus*). Zoo Biol. 11:121-131

Lambiase, J. T., R. P. Amann and J. S. Lindzey. 1972. Aspects of reproductive physiology of male white-tailed deer. *J. Wildl. Manage.* 36:868-875.

Marchinton, R. L., K. L. Johansen and K. V. Miller. 1990. Behavioral components of white-tailed deer scent marking: social and seasonal effects. Pages 295-301 in D. W. MacDonald, D. Muller-Schwarze, and S. E. Natynczuk, eds. *Chemical signals in Vertebrates 5.* Oxford Univ. Press.

Marchinton, R. L., K. V. Miller, R. J. Hamilton and D. C. Guynn. 1990. Quality deer management: biological and social impacts on the herd. Pages 7-15 in C. Kyser, D. C. Sisson and J. L. Landers, eds. Proc, Tall Timbers Game Bird Seminar, Tallahassee, Fla.

Marchinton, R. L., R. J. Hamilton, K. V. Miller, E. L. Marchinton, T. L. Kile and W. Cooper. 1993. Quality deer management: A paradigm for the future? *Quality Whitetails* 1:6-9.

McCullough, D. R. 1979. The George Reserve deer herd. Univ. Michigan Press, Ann Arbor. 271 pp.

Miller, K. V., and R. L. Marchinton. l994. Deer talk: sounds, smells, and postures. (in press) in D. Gerlach, ed. *Deer.* The Stackpole Co., Harrisburg, PA.

Miller, K. V., R. L. Marchinton and W. M. Knox. 1991. White-tailed deer signposts and their role as a source or priming pheromones: a hypothesis. Pages 455-458 in B. Bobek, K, Perzanowski, and W. Regelin, eds. Global trends in wildlife management. Trans. 18th IUGB Congress, Krakow 1987. Swiat Press, Krakow-Warszawa.

Miller, K. V., K. E. Kammermeyer, R. L. Marchinton and B. Moser. 1987. Population and habitat influences on antler rubbing by white-tailed deer. J. Wildl. Manage. 51:62-66.

Miller, K. V., R. L. Marchinton, K. J. Forand and K. L. Johansen. 1987. Dominance, testosterone levels, and scraping activity in a captive herd of white-tailed deer. J. Mammal. 68:812-817.

Miller, K. V., O. E. Rhodes Jr., T. R. Litchfield, M. H. Smith and R. L. Marchinton. 1987. Reproductive charactaeristics of yearling and adult male white-tailed deer. Proc. Annu. Conf. Southeast Assoc. Fish and Wildl. Agencies 41:378-384.

Mirarchi, R. E., P. F. Scanlon and R. L. Kirpatrick. 1977. Annual changes in spermatozoan production and associated organs of white-tailed deer. J. Wildl. Manage. 41:92-99.

Mirarchi, R. E., B. E. Howland, P. F. Scanlon, R. L. Kirkpatrick and L. M. Sanford. 1978. Seasonal variation in plasma, LH, FSH, prolactin and testosterone concentrations in adult male white-tailed deer. Canadian J. Zool. 56:121-127.

Moore, W. G., and R. L. Marchinton. 1974. Marking behavior and its social function in white-tailed deer. Pp. 447-456, in V. Geist and F. Walther, eds. The behaviour of ungulates and its relation to management. Intern. Union of Cons. of Nature Publ. 24:1-511.

Nelson, M. E., and L. D. Mech. 1981. Deer social organization and wolf predation in Northeastern Minnesota. Wildl. Monogr. 77. 53 pp.

Nelson, M. E., and L. D. Mech. 1984. Home-range formation and dispersal of deer in Northeastern Minnesota. J. Mammal. 65: 567-575.

Nielsen, D. G., M. J. Dunlap and K. V. Miller. 1982. Pre-rut rubbing by white-tailed bucks: nursery damage, social role, and management options. Wildl. Soc. Bull. 10:341-348.

Nixon, C. M., L. P. Hansen, P. A. Brewer and J. E. Chelsvig. 1991. Ecology of white-tailed deer in an intensively farmed region of Illinois. Wildl. Monogr. 118. Washington D. C.: The Wildlife Society. 77 pp.

Ozoga, J. J. 1985. Marks of excellence. Michigan Sportsman 10:44 46.

Ozoga, J. J. 1988. Incidence of "infant" antlers among supplementally fed white-tailed deer. J. Mammal. 69:393-395.

Ozoga, J. J. 1989. Temporal pattern of scraping behavior in white-tailed deer. J. Mammal. 70:633-636.

Ozoga, J. J. 1989. Induced scraping activity in white-tailed deer. J. Wildl. Manage. 53:877-880.

Ozoga, J. J. 1994. Competitive signposting. *Deer & Deer Hunting.* 17(7):46-47.

Ozoga, J. J. 1994. Buck rub traits and how to induce rubbing. *Deer & Deer Hunting.* 18(1):16-18, 20, 22, 24-25.

Ozoga, J. J. 1994. The overhead limb—for bucks only. *Deer & Deer Hunting.* 18(2): 16-18, 20-22, 24, 26, 28, 29.

Ozoga, J. J., and L. J. Verme. 1975. Activity patterns of white tailed deer during estrus. J. Wildl. Manage. 39:679-683.

Ozoga, J. J., and L. J. Verme. 1982. Physical and reproductive characteristics of a supplementally fed white-tailed deer herd. J. Wildl. Manage. 46:281-301.

Ozoga, J. J., and L. J. Verme. 1984. Effects of family-bond deprivation on reproductive performance in female white-tailed deer. J. Wildl. Manage. 48:1326-1334.

Ozoga, J. J., and L. J. Verme. 1985. Comparative breeding behavior and performance of yearlings vs. prime-age white tailed bucks. J. Wildl. Manage. 49:364-372.

Ozoga, J. J., and L. J. Verme. 1986. Initial and subsequent maternal success of white-tailed deer. J. Wildl. Manage. 50:122-124.

Peterle, T. J. 1975. Deer sociobiology. Wildl. Soc. Bull. 3: 82-83.

Plotka, E. D., U. S. Seal, M. A. Letellier, L. J. Verme and J. J. Ozoga. 1981. The effect of pinealectomy on seasonal phenotypic changes in white-tailed deer (*Odocoileus virginianus borealis*). Pages 45-56 in C. D. Mathews and R. F. Seamark, eds. Pineal Function. Elsevier North-Holland Biomedical Press.

Plotka, E. D., U. S. Seal, L. J. Verme and J. J. Ozoga. 1977. Reproductive steroids in the white-tailed deer (*Odocoileus virginianus borealis*) II. Progesterone and estrogen levels in peripheral plasma during pregnancy. Biol. Reprod. 17:78-83.

Rue, L. L. III. 1989. The deer of North America. 2nd edition, updated and expanded. Outdoor life books. Grolier Book Clubs Inc. Danbury, Ct. 508 pp.

Sawyer, T. G., R. L. Marchinton and C. W. Bersford. 1982. Scraping behavior in female white-tailed deer. J. Mammal. 63:696-697.

Sawyer, T. G., R. L. Marchinton and K. V. Miller. 1989. Response of female white-tailed deer to scrapes and antler rubs. J. Mammal. 70:431-433.

Sawyer, T. G., K. V. Miller and R. L. Marchinton. 1993. Patterns of urination and rub-urination in female white-tailed deer. J. Mammal. 74:477-479.

Thomas, J. W., R. M. Robinson and R. G. Marburger. 1965. Social behavior in a white-tailed deer herd containing hypogondal males. J. Mammal. 46:314-327.

Townsend, T. W., and E. D. Bailey. 1981. Effects of age, sex, and weight on social rank in penned white-tailed deer. Am. Midl. Nat. 106:92-101.

Verme, L. J. 1965. Reproduction studies on penned white-tailed deer. J. Wildl. Manage. 29:74-79.

Verme, L. J. 1969. Reproductive patterns of white-tailed deer related to nutritional plane. J. Wildl. Manage. 33:881-887.

Verme, L. J. 1983. Sex ratio variations in *Odocoileus:* a critical review. J. Wildl. Manage. 47:573-582.

Verme, L. J., and R. V. Doepker. 1988. Suppression of reproduction in Upper Michigan white-tailed deer, *Odocoileus virginianus*, by climatic stress during the rut. Canadian Field Nat. 102:550-552.

Verme, L. J., and J. J. Ozoga. 1980. Influence of protein-energy intake on deer fawns in autumn. J. Wildl. Manage. 44:305-314.

Verme, L. J., and J. J. Ozoga. 1980. Effect of diet on growth and lipogenesis in deer fawns. J. Wildl. Manage. 44:315-324.

Verme, L. J., and J. J. Ozoga. 1981. Sex ratio of white-tailed deer and the estrus cycle. J. Wildl. Manage. 45:710-715.

Verme, L. J., and J. J. Ozoga. 1987. Relationships of photoperiod to puberty in doe fawn white-tailed deer. J. Mammal. 68:107-110.

Verme, L. J., J. J. Ozoga and J. T. Nellist. 1987. Induced early estrus in penned white-tailed deer. J. Wildl. Manage. 51:54-56.

Warren, R. J., R. W. Vogelsang, R. L. Kirpatrick and P. F. Scanlon. 1978. Reproductive behavior of captive white-tailed deer. Animal Behav. 26:179-183.

Whitney, M. D., D. L. Forester, K. V. Miller and R. L. Marchinton. 1991. Sexual attraction in white-tailed deer. Pages 327-333 in R. D. Brown, ed. The biology of deer. Springer-Verlag.

Woods, G. R., R. J. Hamilton, D. C. Guynn, R. L. Marchinton and K. V. Miller. 1993. How whitetails use traditional rubs. *Deer & Deer Hunting* 17(4):30-36.